ENDORSEMENTS

The KLAS Research EHR Interoperability Report 2024 found that healthcare organizations often feel unempowered to improve interoperability for their clinicians and patients. In this book, Harm Scherpbier lays out the steps forward to more interoperability and more multivendor IT environments, creating a better experience for patients and clinicians.

—ADAM GALE
Founder and CEO, KLAS Research

Scherpbier lays out a compelling and pragmatic vision for unleashing a true productivity revolution in healthcare delivery—by opening up health data and enabling consumer and clinician application access to a competitive marketplace of products and services. There is no other way to realize the promise of a more connected and collaborative public/private healthcare system!

—ANEESH CHOPRA
Former US chief technology officer (2009–2012); author of *Innovative State: How New Technologies Can Transform Government*

Harm Scherpbier wears many hats—that of a physician, a chief medical information officer, a healthcare informaticist, and a software developer. So no one is more informed on the issue of the health IT "monoculture" than Harm who makes the case for health-tech diversity, dynamism, and flexibility in *Unvendor*. As Todd Park, former chief technology officer of the US under the Obama administration, proposed "Data liberación!" for healthcare back in 2011, Harm argues for "Health IT liberación!" in 2025.

—JANE SARASOHN-KAHN, MA, MHSA
THINK-Health and the *Health Populi* blog

In a rapidly changing healthcare ecosystem, we are asking non-traditional providers to perform their duties in non-traditional settings with non-traditional compensation schemes and outcome measures. Traditional EHRs were never designed with these priorities in mind. With over thirty-five years of experience as a doctor, IT vendor, CMIO, teacher, and health information exchange expert, Dr. Scherpbier's perspectives are both welcome and timely. They are compellingly laid out in *Unvendor: Innovate Healthcare with a Diverse IT Stack*.

—KIP WEBB, MD, MPH
Pediatrician; adjunct faculty, UC Berkeley School of Public Health

Harm Scherpbier, a longtime leader in health information technology, is in the kitchen cooking with gas. I learned that you should not put all of your IT eggs in one basket. Also, be prepared to crack some eggs to make a healthy omelet for the future! Translation: the era of the single vendor is over, and I say good riddance. The future is here, and Scherpbier is writing it now.

—DAVID B. NASH, MD, MBA
Founding dean emeritus, Dr. Raymond C. and Doris N. Grandon Professor of Health Policy, Jefferson College of Population Health, Philadelphia, Pennsylvania

In the rapidly evolving landscape of healthcare, the agility of our technology stack is not just important—it's essential. Health systems must harness emerging technologies to revolutionize our workforce, elevate quality, and enhance patient outcomes. Relying on a single vendor for all clinical healthcare IT needs is not only unsustainable but also breeds monopolistic inefficiency. True innovation cannot be monopolized; it demands a diverse, adaptable approach to meet the challenges of tomorrow and deliver the exceptional care our communities deserve.

—EVE CUNNINGHAM, MD, MBA

Chief of Virtual Care and Digital Health, Providence

Harm Scherpbier encourages us to rethink the singular vendor IT stack as a way to promote and stimulate meaningful innovation. A diverse IT stack is a core ingredient, and one of several essential ingredients, to allow for transformational leaps forward in an ever-changing healthcare and technology landscape. This book points the way toward IT-supported healthcare innovation.

—RASU SHRESTHA, MD, MBA

Chief innovation and commercialization officer, Advocate Health

UNVENDOR

HARM SCHERPBIER, MD

UNVENDOR

INNOVATE HEALTHCARE
WITH A DIVERSE IT STACK

Advantage | Books

Published by Advantage Books, Charleston, South Carolina.
An imprint of Advantage Media.

ADVANTAGE is a registered trademark, and the Advantage colophon is a trademark of Advantage Media Group, Inc.

Printed in the United States of America.

10 9 8 7 6 5 4 3 2 1

ISBN: 979-8-89188-167-9 (Paperback)
ISBN: 979-8-89188-168-6 (eBook)

Library of Congress Control Number: 2025900541

Book design by Megan Elger.

This publication is designed to provide accurate and authoritative information in regard to the subject matter covered. It is sold with the understanding that the publisher is not engaged in rendering legal, accounting, or other professional services. If legal advice or other expert assistance is required, the services of a competent professional person should be sought.

Advantage Books is an imprint of Advantage Media Group. Advantage Media helps busy entrepreneurs, CEOs, and leaders write and publish a book to grow their business and become the authority in their field. Advantage authors comprise an exclusive community of industry professionals, idea-makers, and thought leaders. For more information go to **advantagemedia.com**.

CONTENTS

ABOUT THE AUTHOR

DR. HARM SCHERPBIER is a physician, born and raised in the Netherlands, where he completed his medical training at the University of Groningen. During his medical training, he became fascinated by computers and information systems, and how these systems might help make healthcare better, more efficient, and more user-friendly. He pursued a master's degree in medical informatics from the Erasmus University Rotterdam and devoted his career to health information technology.

Harm is a health IT strategy advisor partnering with firms on clinical system development, population health solutions, data analytics, and health IT implementation and strategy. He is the chief medical information officer at HealthShare Exchange, the Philadelphia regional Health Information Exchange, focusing on expanding the reach and relevance of the information exchange in clinical care and population health. He teaches health informatics and population health analytics at the Jefferson College of Population Health in Philadelphia, Pennsylvania. He is a fellow of the Health Information Management Systems Society (HIMSS), a member of the HIMSS Physician Committee and the Interoperability Committee, and a fellow of the American Medical Informatics Association, where he is a core team member of the Health Informatics Accreditation program.

Dr. Scherpbier was previously chief medical information officer at Main Line Health, a five-hospital integrated health network near Philadelphia, where he was responsible for the implementation of healthcare information systems and electronic patient records for physicians, nurses, and other clinicians throughout the health system. He worked in software engineering and product management teams at Shared Medical Systems, Siemens Health Services, CareScience, Aetna US Healthcare, eClinicalWorks, and Philips Wellcentive.

Harm and his wife, Titia, live in the suburbs of Philadelphia, Pennsylvania. They love spending time outdoors with their kids, going hiking, camping, biking, skiing, or kayaking in beautiful places.

INTRODUCTION

T he US healthcare system is changing fast, and these changes force health providers to be agile, responsive, and able to deal with new payment models, new care models, and new technologies. Together, these converging forces compel healthcare stakeholders to do more with less, and to take a new digital health approach.

In most hospitals and large physician practices in the US, you'll find information technology (IT) from a single health IT vendor. The single-vendor approach dominates the health IT market, creating IT monocultures within large healthcare organizations: all information systems from one IT firm with very few other systems or system components in the mix. There are benefits to a single-vendor IT infrastructure—for example, the reduced need to manage connections and data exchange between various systems. But there are also downsides. It is time that we question the single-vendor mentality and diversify our health IT environments, reduce our dependency on a single IT megavendor, and bring other information technologies, from other firms, into the organization. There are three health IT megavendors in the US: Epic, Oracle Health (previously Cerner), and Meditech. Each has a different technology foundation, different market segment and client base, and a different style of working with their customers. All three aim to become the single health IT vendor to your hospital or health system, where they deliver the billing system, the registration system, the electronic health record (EHR), the emergency department (ED) system, the lab and radiology systems, and the pharmacy system. They become your monoculture vendor.

I believe now it's time to unvendor®,[1] to steer away from the single-vendor strategy, to create a more diverse health IT stack, so our healthcare organizations become more innovative, flexible, and competitive.

Our healthcare organizations need to be competitive, nimble, and up to date, as changes are coming at us from multiple directions:

- *Payment models* continue to shift from traditional fee-for-service healthcare to quality- and value-based healthcare models.

- *Care models* aim to move patients away from expensive acute care settings toward care in ambulatory and subacute settings and to the patient's home. There is a strong trend toward "hospital-at-home care," using technologies to connect the patient at home to the providers in the healthcare organization as well as to community- and retail-based health service providers (e.g., retail pharmacy, grocery stores for medical food delivery).

- *New technologies* emerge, not just in healthcare but in other industries, and healthcare providers need to take advantage of the most useful of these technologies to make their organizations competitive, and to be able to hire and retain the best staff. Examples of new technologies waiting to become part of the health IT fabric are artificial intelligence (AI)/ machine learning (ML) applications, robotic process automation (RPA) and workflow management systems, and remote

---

1   Registered in the US Patent and Trademark Office.

sensoring/remote patient monitoring technologies. These new technologies will not come from the health IT megavendors. Healthcare providers must work with other technology firms to incorporate these systems into their organizations.

- *Changing user experiences* (UXs) from clinicians and patients alike. Clinicians experience burnout and frustration from the use of EHRs. Patients and health consumers require a better experience in their interaction with your physicians and nurses, and with your organization.

Health provider organizations need to shift their mindset from a single-vendor everything-under-one-roof mentality to a technology-diverse, interconnected set of applications, with the ability to rapidly respond to changes by phasing out old technologies and replacing them with newer, state-of-the-art components. We need to move away from reliance on one single IT vendor and embrace a mix of technologies. A health IT ecosystem with components from multiple vendors, connected via modern interoperability tools, offers agility, a wider range of options for users, and a platform for clinical service improvement and competitiveness.

In the 1980s, most hospitals installed systems from multiple companies, interconnected through interfaces. We called it the "best-of-breed" concept—buy the best system on the market for each sector in your hospital and connect them through interfaces. In the 1990s, the market shifted from best of breed to single vendor and never looked back.

In this book, we will briefly explore how and why the landscape shifted toward the current single-vendor culture, up to now, and how we can (need to!) push the pendulum back toward a more diverse health IT ecosystem. We'll explore the benefits of integrating other components into your health system, and we will outline the steps from your current single-vendor state to a more diverse and modular IT environment. We will also discuss the obstacles and challenges on this road—and how to overcome those barriers.

During my career I have played on both sides of the health IT fence. I worked as a physician advisor for large health IT vendors and also served as chief medical information officer (CMIO) at a five-hospital health system, during the "meaningful use" years, enjoying the incentive-driven momentum for EHR implementations for hospitals and physician practices. I will admit that I advocated for the single-vendor approach, simultaneously realizing there were limitations to it. I also worked as CMIO for a health information exchange (HIE) organization, giving me an entirely new perspective on the need for interoperability, for data exchange, for looking outside your health organization's single-vendor walls. In the chapters ahead, I'll share my stories and insights with you and show you how I am now firmly back on the unvendor side—for innovation, competitiveness, user engagement, and a more dynamic and resilient healthcare environment.

I have nothing against IT vendors. They are doing what they have to do—sell more software, encourage you to spend every last health IT budget dollar with them instead of competitors. It isn't their fault. No, the latch is on the inside; we need to unlock our own door. It will be up to the clients, the customers, the consumers of healthcare IT, to detach themselves from the large vendor and to bring in a variety of new and innovative solutions.

This book is for leaders and executives in healthcare organizations: chief information officers (CIOs), CMIOs, chief nursing information officers (CNIOs), and also their chief medical officers (CMOs), chief nursing officers (CNOs), chief executive officers (CEOs), and chief financial officers (CFOs). I believe that the entire C-suite plays a role in the unvendor project, and the entire C-suite will benefit with better care, better competitiveness, more innovation, happier users, more engaged patients, and lower health IT bills.

I also wrote this book for the many small and midsize health IT firms, with innovative products, who are running into closed doors and closed minds. The response to a start-up health IT company is often, "We checked with our vendor; they say it's on their road map." In other words, "I don't want to buy this from you now. I'd rather wait until my megavendor has figured out that they need this feature or function." The road map ends up more like a frustrating roadblock to up-and-coming health IT vendors. I hope my call to unvendor will also result in more opportunities for innovative companies and a thriving health IT industry.

Who Will Make the First Move?

Healthcare is a team sport. Running a health system is also a team sport. Any player in the team can make the first move and take the initiative to unvendor.

If you're the CIO, you are responsible for IT infrastructure. You need to be strategic and risk-averse at the same time. You can't afford any security glitches or malware attacks. However, you are also responsible for a cutting-edge technology system that keeps your organization innovative and competitive in a changing market. In addition, you need to build platform redundancy to be prepared and strategically positioned for significant vendor system changes. You're in a first-mover position.

If you're the CMIO or CNIO, it's your primary responsibility to help doctors and nurses use the EHR to deliver patient care, effectively and efficiently. There is an ongoing concern about burnout among physicians and nurses, partially caused by the "friction" brought by the EHR, and aggravated by the COVID-19 pandemic, mental and behavioral health crises, and staff shortages. Technology needs to make work better and easier. If traditional EHRs don't make work better and easier, it's the CMIO's and CNIO's role to introduce solutions and technologies. You need to look beyond your IT megavendor to evaluate clinical workflow tools and technologies and consider unvendor choices.

If you're the CMO or CNO, you are in charge and responsible for the clinical workforce in your organization—the physicians, nurses, and other clinicians. How does your organization create the best work environment and experience for your staff? IT plays a major role in how clinicians work, determining their effectiveness and efficiency. But beyond the clinical staff, you're also responsible for your patients' experience. Patients are exposed to health IT either indirectly—when their physician or nurse is working on the EHR with their eyes on the screen and not on the patient—or directly, as users of the patient portal that's now a standard and required component in every EHR. As a CMO or CNO, you can be the first mover to introduce technologies from outside vendors to boost the quality of care, the clinician experience, and patient satisfaction.

If you're the CEO or chief operating officer (COO), you drive the healthcare organization's excellence and competitiveness. While you're one step removed from technology decisions (in the hands of the CIO, CMIO, and CNIO), you should worry that all your technology comes from one kitchen and that this one kitchen cannot be up to date and cutting edge on every emerging healthcare need and technology innovation. CEOs need to support their IT teams by encouraging and demanding IT diversity, and promoting tools outside the typical health IT shopping list. Strive to be the unvendor first mover by requiring emerging technologies and connected third-party components.

If you're the CFO, you are responsible for the bottom line, both for this year and ten or twenty years from now. While the primary concern may be the cost of the EHR and IT, you also worry about the cost of care delivery and the role of IT in increasing care efficiencies. CFOs should support unvendoring for two reasons: first, a dispassionate approach to the cost of their single health IT megavendor and the ability to bring in competing, advanced components to extend and eventually replace the single system. Secondly, and more importantly, a leader needs to include tools that directly increase care efficiency: workflow optimization, RPA, AI/ML tools geared at identifying wasteful practices, tools that can keep patients in their home settings, and more. These tools will likely not come from the single vendor, so a broader mix of technologies will ultimately help the CFO's mission. CFOs can be powerful first movers in the leadership team.

Each of the players above has a reason to unvendor, and each has their own specific contribution to the unvendor project. Weaning your organization off single-vendor dependency is a difficult task that demands the entire leadership team get involved.

This book is not a diatribe against large health IT vendors. On the contrary, as we'll discuss in a later chapter, large IT vendors have been tremendously successful in automating and digitizing every aspect of the health system. It's the IT vendor's job to expand their footprint and be strong in every market segment. In the opening chapter, we will examine how megavendors were so successful in expanding their systems into all departments in the healthcare organizations. To unvendor doesn't mean eliminating the vendor but **reducing the dependency on a single IT vendor** to actively create diversity in tools and technologies, to bring components in and out of the healthcare workflow. The large health IT vendor provides the platform for all base functionality in the healthcare organization as a backbone for innovative and connected technologies.

Unvendoring diversifies the health IT portfolio. It means creating a more agile and responsive IT environment to keep up with changes in reimbursement, care processes, patient expectations, and technology trends. It means investing in a broader range of technologies as a risk-mitigation strategy. It means building a competitive IT environment that powers and enables your organization's care team and processes. Unvendoring shifts from an IT monoculture into an adaptable, diversified system benefiting patients, providers, and staff, and thus the entire healthcare organization.

It is the responsibility of health system leaders (CIOs, CMIOs/ CNIOs, CMOs/CNOs, CEOs, and others) to shift our health systems away from dependence on single large EHR vendors. This book lays out the reasons and rationale for doing so, and the pathway toward technology diversity. Unvendoring is a necessary step, in the short term, for innovation and health system responsiveness, and in the longer term, as the groundwork toward an entirely new EHR ecosystem. It starts with unvendoring, and it's up to our C-suite teams to make the first moves.

A final point: I don't intend this book to be a lecture, a sermon, a white paper, or sage advice. Nobody needs that. I would like this book to be the start of a conversation and the beginning of a long-term project, which we can do together: to transition from the current state of health IT into the next phase. We don't know exactly what that next phase will look like, but I would like to partner with you on the journey and hear about what your organization is doing to evolve your health IT ecosystem. I want to hear about success and failures so we can learn from both. What are your team's top priorities and how can I help you in your next steps? It is my intention to open dialogue and share feedback with anyone ready to unvendor!

I would love to hear your unvendor stories and experiences. Please share them with me at unvendor.us or at harm@scherpbier.health.

PART ONE

HOW DID WE GET HERE?

Why do we call our IT firms "vendors"? It's a strange word. I associate the term *vendor* with a food truck, a guy hawking beers or popcorn at a sports game, or someone selling merchandise outside the stadium. Research and advisory firm Gartner explains the term vendor as the "last entity in the chain that brands a product and sells it directly to end users or through a channel."[2] Investopedia explains the term vendor broadly as "anyone who sells goods or services," and further clarifies that the vendor "can operate as both a supplier (or seller) of goods and a manufacturer."[3]

I think the use of the word "vendor" for health IT firms comes from the early days of healthcare computing when many health systems in the US built their own systems. Those early systems were called "homegrown." Sophisticated EHRs didn't exist yet in the market, so some of the major hospitals coded their own. Examples of health systems with homegrown systems were Intermountain Health LDS Hospital in Salt Lake City,

---

2   Gartner Information Technology Glossary, accessed November 11, 2024, https://www.gartner.com/en/information-technology/glossary/vendor.

3   Mitchell Grant, "What Is a Vendor? Definition, Types, and Example," Investopedia, June 13, 2024, https://www.investopedia.com/terms/v/vendor.asp.

Utah, with their HELP system, and the Regenstrief Institute in India-napolis, Indiana, with their eponymous Regenstrief system. Vanderbilt University Medical Center (Tennessee), Massachusetts General Hospital, Brigham and Women's Hospital (Massachusetts), and many other large hospitals had homegrown early versions of EHRs. Though they are now transitioning to a commercial EHR, the Veterans Health Administration hospitals use a homegrown health information system, called VistA.

Over time, hospitals with homegrown systems had to hire and employ teams of programmers to keep their EHRs running and continue to add new functionality to respond to their users' needs. It became more difficult and costly to maintain a homegrown system and to keep the system up to date on current technology. This led hospitals to gradually introduce system components from IT firms—marking the transition from homegrown to vendor systems. The first "vendor" systems in these organizations were patient registration and patient accounting, with the major players in the market being Shared Medical Systems (SMS) and HBO & Co. (HBOC), which became McKesson HBOC after a merger. Later, vendors emerged with com-mercially viable EHRs. Homegrown systems could not keep up with technology trends, modern user interfaces, and the growing needs of clinical users. Today, I am not aware of a single homegrown EHR left, as all hospitals and health systems use "vendors."

The state of the EHR market today is four or five firms providing commercial acute care EHRs, and a much larger number of firms with EHRs for primary care or specialty practices. That's the starting point for this book, and the beginning of the unvendor journey.

CHAPTER 1

HOW DID WE GET TO SINGLE-VENDOR DOMINANCE?

Most US health systems and healthcare provider organizations use IT from a single large vendor providing the EHR, patient accounting, general ledgers, lab results, radiology and pharmacy reports, as well as decision support (DS) and analytics. We will discuss how the three large health IT vendor firms became so successful in powering US health systems—and why other firms didn't make it to "megavendor" status. But first, how did we get to the point that most health systems have a technology stack from one vendor only?

In these early days of vendor-supported IT solutions, hospitals would install systems from multiple vendors, following the best-of-breed approach discussed in the introduction. The thinking was to purchase the best system on the market for a specific hospital function—patient accounting, lab, radiology, pharmacy, EHR, order entry, etc.—and connect them via interfaces.

Out of the best-of-breed philosophy emerged the Health Level 7 (HL7) organization standards to help standardize the interfaces required to keep these systems talking to each other. At the core of a best-of-breed system was an interface engine, managing the communications between the various systems.

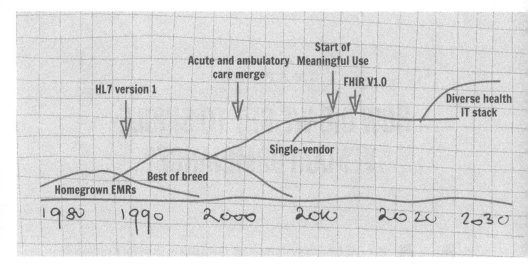

Figure 1: Timeline of health IT trends and technologies

The best-of-breed approach fell out of favor when hospitals struggled with managing multiple systems from a variety of vendors, demanding constant interface updates, maintenance, and troubleshooting. Not only was this a matter of IT staff burden and workload, but there were also patient safety issues, with potential information loss between interfaced systems. The pendulum swung away from best-of-breed systems to single-vendor solutions, with all system components coming from a single vendor and not requiring the setup and maintenance of interfaces between subsystems. Today, most hospitals and health systems deploy information systems from a single vendor, with most or all modules coming from one company and driven from one database, without the need to link subsystems via HL7 interfaces. Patient registration, patient accounting, order management, the EHR, laboratory, radiology, and pharmacy are all components coming from a single vendor. A single-vendor health IT environment is easier to maintain, and it reduces patient safety concerns.

The benefits of the single-vendor approach are clear and well documented:[4, 5]

- Fewer interfaces and connections between systems, which reduces the effort and spending to keep interfaces running and up to date, and to maintain them during system upgrades.

- Fewer contracts to manage and fewer IT companies to work with. If there is a software issue, hospitals don't have several parties pointing fingers at one another; it's just one phone call to a single vendor.[6]

- Patient safety concerns: Fewer connections and fewer points of data exchange mean lower risk of errors in transactions that might result in mistakes in patient registrations, orders, results, or other clinical data flows.

- Users find it easier to do all their work in one system, rather than switching to different systems for different tasks.

- Data security: With fewer software components in the mix, it may be more difficult for hackers to gain access to the data and cause a data breach or malware attack.

---

4   Hanadi Y. Hamadi et al., "Single-Vendor Electronic Health Record Use Is Associated with Greater Opportunities for Organizational and Clinical Care Improvements," *Mayo Clinic Proceedings: Innovations, Quality & Outcomes* 6, no. 3 (June 2022): 269–78, https://doi.org/10.1016/j.mayocpiqo.2022.05.001.

5   K. Wowak et al., "Strategic Sourcing of Multicomponent Software Systems: The Case of Electronic Medical Records," *Decision Sciences* 55, no. 3 (June 2024): 227–44, https://doi.org/10.1111/deci.12576.

6   K. Brimmer, "Hospitals Can Gain Time and Money with Single-Vendor Distribution," Healthcare Finance News, May 31, 2012, https://www.healthcarefinancenews.com/news/hospitals-can-gain-time-and-money-single-vendor-distribution.

I'm not going to argue that these benefits aren't real because it's impossible to make the case that an organization with a wide variety of clinical systems can deliver better care at lower costs. There are significant benefits to a single health IT platform, but they come with their own limitations and downsides to the single-vendor approach:[7]

- High cost. The vendor will argue that you're saving money by purchasing all systems in a single bundle from one vendor rather than purchasing components from multiple vendors. It's well known that the health IT megavendors charge astronomical rates for their software. In chapter 4 we will look in more detail at pricing and the single-vendor chokehold.

- Innovation delay. Healthcare changes often, with new care delivery methods, new payment and reimbursement models, and new patient engagement and consumer-facing technologies. The large IT vendors are slow in responding to healthcare changes. Niche vendors will have solutions on the market well before the large vendor, while a single-vendor approach significantly delays the ability to deploy innovative solutions. Examples are rapid implementation of value-based care (VBC), hospital-at-home and remote patient monitoring, vendor-agnostic patient portals, and more.

- Forced workflow uniformity. While there are benefits to having all users on the same system, using the same workflows and user interfaces, this also creates inefficiencies and user dissatisfaction. A hospital or a health system has a large variety of skills, workflow requirements, and specialty needs. Strict

---

7   R. Koppel and C. Lehmann, "Implications of an Emerging EHR Monoculture for Hospitals and Healthcare Systems," *J Am Med Inform Assoc* 22 (2015): 465–71, https://doi.org/10.1136/amiajnl-2014-003023.

adherence to a single IT vendor serving all users and all roles eliminates the flexibility to implement niche systems focused on specific workers or groups of workers.

- Single point of failure risk/all eggs in one basket. Every IT vendor reaches a point of plateau, and all vendors become obsolete at some point. In a single-vendor setting, a health IT vendor failure, either sudden or slow, will affect all departments and all users. A multivendor technology stack makes a vendor transition easier, more gradual, and typically timelier.

Megavendor Strategies

Before we go into unvendor strategies of moving toward a more diverse and agile health IT stack, we should first understand the mechanisms that caused the major health IT vendors to go from "vendor" to "megavendor." How did a handful of large EHR vendors become megavendors, dominating our healthcare organizations?

This did not happen overnight, and, as we'll see, the path from vendor to megavendor involves very specific steps. Epic is the inventor and pioneer of these megavendor strategies, and the other large health IT firms (Oracle Health/Cerner, Meditech) have attempted to copy these steps with mixed success.

First and foremost: one patient, one record. Before Epic, a hospital EHR was not the same as an ambulatory practice EHR. They were different software systems, usually from different firms. Epic was the first to realize the opportunity to create a single EHR for inpatient, ambulatory, and emergency care, with a single patient record spanning the various care settings. There are many ambulatory EHR companies that haven't reached megavendor status because they can't deliver acute care. All hospitals and health systems today deliver acute, ambulatory, and emergency care, and a single EHR spanning all settings is critical for efficient care delivery.

Epic, as the most successful megavendor, also employs market-growth strategies to grow their regional presence:

- Focus on universities and training hospitals. Most US universities and training institutions use Epic's EHR. The graduating physicians, nurses, and healthcare administrators will move on to work in one of the many US hospitals and health systems. Some of them end up on an EHR selection committee, and they will remember Epic from their early days in training.

- Create a data-sharing network. Epic's Care Everywhere is a proprietary secure network to share patient data between healthcare organizations. Care Everywhere makes it easy and fast to see a patient's clinical data from other regional hospitals. This creates pressure on hospitals to also select Epic as their EHR, so they are able to benefit from the data exchange with other Epic hospitals. This is fear-of-missing-out strategy number one.

- Another fear-of-missing-out strategy is creating a strong following among health IT professionals. This is a more personal strategy, and while all megavendors employ this method, Epic is the most successful. Using their national user's group through meetings and events, and via regional collaborations, Epic is not just an EHR but a community and peer group for many CIOs, CMIOs, and CNIOs. Having an Epic EHR becomes part of an organization's identity and self-esteem.

Finally, there is the pricing strategy, and this is the strongest tool in the toolbox: all-in pricing. With an all-in price, the megavendor offers their entire product suite for a single price, which is usually based on the size of the health system (by revenue, by beds, and/or by number of providers). The ability to offer all-in pricing obviously first requires that the vendor has products in all departments: the EHR system needs to cover registration, EHR for all settings (ambulatory, acute, and emergency care), and all departments (lab, radiology, pharmacy, operating room), analytics, patient portal, etc. The main health IT megavendors in the US have modules in all these spaces, and therefore can offer contracts with all-in pricing.

The all-in contract is very attractive to the client: it's an all-you-can-eat buffet for every health IT need, and it allows the organization to eliminate many other systems and contracts. There are far fewer interfaces, fewer disparate systems, fewer contracts, and fewer systems for the users to oversee. Packaged conveniently, it's an easy sell for all involved and hard to pass up.

There are, however, strong downsides to all-in contracts: By their very design, they crowd out competing systems from other vendors, and so create an internal monopoly. Once a hospital or health system is host to a monopolizing health IT vendor, it locks the organization's strategy tightly to their health IT partner.

- No contracts to smaller "niche" systems—for example, population health systems, analytics and business intelligence (BI) systems, clinical documentation tools, or any third-party modules. The money is spent on the megavendor, which will offer an equivalent module under the all-in price. A separate vendor can't compete with something that the hospital "already owns and has paid for."

- For any new or emerging functionality, where the megavendor does not have a solution in place, the vendor will state that this solution is "on the road map" and will anticipate availability "within the upcoming twelve to twenty-four months." This is industry code for "We don't have it, but we don't want you to buy it from another firm, so we're stalling for time and keeping the competition away." Be aware of the "road map"—a classic stall tactic for monopolizing megavendors.

- Finally, all-in pricing creates long-term dependence on the megavendor. Health systems love the single-vendor approach because there are fewer contracts to manage and fewer support teams involved. In health IT lingo, "one throat to choke." But in the course of time, the situation reverses. The megavendor is in charge, and your throat is the one being choked, by complete dependency on the single vendor. The health system has to swallow whatever pricing the vendor puts forward and has no ability to consider competing systems from other vendors. All-in pricing takes away the ability to negotiate better contracts.

Single-vendor dominance in healthcare is not unique to the US. In the Netherlands, my original home base, hospitals feel locked in by their software vendor ChipSoft. The firm had a 46 percent profit margin in 2018 and tried to block the publication of a critical report on their business practices.[8] Making excessive profits on healthcare services, which are largely funded through public funds and patient insurance premiums, is frowned upon in Europe.

The industry must move away from single-vendor dependency and, despite the all-in pricing contract, start introducing modules from other IT firms into the organization's health IT stack. To unvendor

---

8   Lisa van Lonkhuyzen, "Ziekenhuizen voelen zich klemgezet door software-bouwer," NRC Handelsblad, May 2022, www.nrc.nl/nieuws/2022/05/04/ziekenhuizen-voelen-zich-klemgezet-door-softwarebouwer.

brings back best-of-breed modules where appropriate, allowing an organization to react quicker to healthcare changes and market changes, and, most importantly, leverage the ability to negotiate contract pricing with the main health IT firm.

It's hard to kick the habit, but in the long run, organizations that unvendor will benefit from greater agility, strategic innovations, and a more competitive health IT environment.

Monopoly vs. Monoculture

Koppel and Lehmann wrote, "Epic is replacing other EHR vendors in the market and is beginning to establish a single-vendor landscape, a monoculture" and later, in the same paper, stated, "Epic is creating an emerging monopoly in the USA."[9] A monoculture is not the same as a monopoly, but both have an element of exclusion of competing firms and products.

Epic's US market share is estimated at 39 percent of client hospitals.[10] By revenue, Oracle/Cerner is the largest EHR firm with a 2021 revenue of $5.7 billion[11] (prior to the acquisition by Oracle), compared with Epic's $4.6 billion 2022 revenue.[12] The number three player in the acute care hospital market is Meditech, with 16 percent

---

9   R. Koppel and C. Lehmann, "Implications of an Emerging EHR Monoculture for Hospitals and Healthcare Systems," *J Am Med Inform Assoc* 22 (2015): 465–71, https://doi.org/10.1136/amiajnl-2014-003023.

10   Naomi Diaz, "Epic's Market Share Throughout the Years," Becker Hospital Review, May 20, 2024, https://www.beckershospitalreview.com/ehrs/ epics-market-share-throughout-the-years.

11   Statista, "Annual Revenue of Cerner 2014–2021," September 27, 2023, https://www. statista.com/statistics/1073319/annual-revenue-of-cerner-corp.

12   Giles Bruce, "Epic's Revenue by Year," Becker's Health IT, December 2023, https:// www.beckershospitalreview.com/ehrs/epics-revenue-by-year.

of hospitals,[13] primarily in the smaller hospital sector, with annual revenue of $0.5B in 2023.[14] By these measures, neither Oracle/Cerner nor Epic look like a monopoly, with sufficient competition in the market, more so when you consider the ambulatory EHR space, with many EHR companies and a highly fragmented market.

Looking at regional trends, there are specific areas in the US that show signs of an Epic monoculture: many health organizations use Epic's EHR, and as more come on board it becomes increasingly likely that neighboring systems will also choose Epic. Examples of regional Epic monoculture are in place in Boston, Chicago, Philadelphia, San Francisco, and Seattle—all cities with multiple large healthcare organizations dominated by Epic's EHR. This monoculture trend is driven by the ability to share data using Epic's Care Everywhere network, the ability to attract physicians and nurses familiar with the system and, to some extent, regional prestige.

There may not be a national market monopoly—yet. But it exists at the regional level and clearly, internally. An internal monopoly means that one company monopolizes all health IT business in a large health system, provides the lion's share of health IT function, and is responsible for the majority of the health system's IT budget, while pushing all competing vendors and IT firms out of the organization.

An internal monopoly stifles a health system's ability to innovate, respond, and react to healthcare changes, and robs users of a better experience. Health systems today are highly dependent on their IT vendors, who have a stranglehold on their clients, and the solution is to unvendor.

---

13 Giles Bruce, "EHR Vendor Market Share in the US," Becker's Health IT, May 2023, https://www.beckershospitalreview.com/ehrs/ehr-vendor-market-share-in-the-us.html.

14 Zippia, "MEDITECH Revenue: Annual, Quarterly, and Historic–Zippia," July 21, 2023, https://www.zippia.com/medical-information-technology-careers-30915/revenue/.

As EHRs have evolved over the past forty years, there are some key takeaways:

- During the best-of-breed phase, hospitals bought components from various health IT firms and linked them together using interface engines and HL7 interfaces.

- HL7 standards emerged to support best-of-breed systems interoperability.

- Single-vendor systems replaced best-of-breed systems, driven by the need for consistent and reliable data availability, and the cost and effort of maintaining many interfaces. Large EHR vendors locked clients into a single-vendor approach through strong functionality across the board, and all-in pricing.

- Fast Healthcare Interoperability Resources (FHIR)[15] standards emerged to support modular interoperability between systems and apps, enabling a more diverse health IT stack. More about this in chapter 6.

- Single-vendor systems provide benefits to the organization: easier maintenance, fewer contracts, consistent IT architecture, and potentially fewer access points for security failures and data breaches. On the other hand, single-vendor systems create a complete dependency on the IT vendor.

- Diverse health IT stacks give organizations more flexibility, innovation, and responsiveness. They can also reduce the overall cost of health IT and result in a more secure data environment.

---

15   "Introduction," HL7 FHIR, March 26, 2023, https://www.hl7.org/fhir/overview.html.

In the next chapter, we will discuss how healthcare is changing, and how this places new demands on your organization's IT. Your health IT system is your organization's central nervous system, determining how patients flow through your organization, how your staff members communicate, and how operations are coordinated. Changing how your organization works means changing your information system. Actually, it's even stronger: any change in your health system's operations starts by changing your IT system, the mechanism to change.

Workbook

How do you see the current and possible future state of your organization's health IT systems? Whether you work for a large health system or a small to midsize practice, your IT influences how your team works, and how your patients interact with you. Let's look at the properties that characterize your IT environment.

Tom Miller, former CEO of Siemens Health Services, referred to the properties and characteristics of a health IT system as "-ilities"— dependability, reliability, affordability, usability, flexibility, performance, and security (a couple "non-ilities" slipped in there). Table 1 below shows how a single-vendor IT compares to a more diverse health IT stack, using a scale of 1 (worst) to 5 (best).

Use the current state column to rank your organization's IT environment. The desired future state column indicates where you would like to see improvements over time.

Table 1. Using -ilities to score health IT systems

"-ILITY"— SYSTEM CHARACTERISTIC OR PROPERTY	SINGLE VENDOR	DIVERSE HEALTH IT STACK	YOUR CURRENT STATE	YOUR DESIRED FUTURE STATE
Functionality	4	5		
Usability—staff	3	5		
Usability—patients and clients	3	4		
Reliability	4— all or nothing	4— fewer single points of failure		
Maintenance and service	4	3		
Affordability	2	2 then 3— higher cost initially, then lower		
Data security, system security	5	4		
Resilience	4	5		
Interoperability/data exchange	3	5		
Innovation	3	5		
Futureproof	3	5		
Competitiveness	3	5		
Flexibility	3	5		
ADD ANY OTHER -ILITIES THAT ARE RELEVANT TO YOUR TEAM HERE				

Now we have a sense of our current IT environment and where we'd like to be in three, five, or ten years. It's difficult to predict what healthcare will look like in a decade, but unvendoring should be the goal. The challenge is to improve the "-ilities" in your columns with a five-to-ten-year horizon in mind.

PART TWO

WHY DO WE CARE?

After I graduated from medical school, in Holland, I planned to start a neurology residency. I loved how neurology integrates with behavior, movement and action, sensors and reaction, and communication. I was especially fascinated by how the central nervous system acts as the control center while the peripheral nervous system sends signals to and from every part of the body.

During my study years in the 1980s, I also did a lot of computer research work involving brain signals. Our research team placed tiny electrodes into rats' brains to try to identify the source of brain waves, the pacemaker of the brain. I don't think we ever found it (it may not exist), but I enjoyed the programming and signal-processing work, which required substantial computing power. This interest in computers and information systems led me to pursue a degree in medical informatics, an entirely new field in the late '80s and early '90s.

Health IT is really the neurology of the organization, so in hindsight, the change wasn't so far fetched. Health information systems determine how the organization works, how team members communicate, and how patients interact with the organization. It drives how everything in the hospital works: how a physician orders tests and medications for a patient, how the pharmacy delivers these medications, how the nurses administer the medications, and how the accounting team bills the insurance company for the medications. Every action and every communication today works its way through the information system in the hospital or medical practice. And just as the nervous system controls how a body operates and communicates, the IT system determines how an organization functions top to bottom.

Health IT isn't just another piece of technology. It's the essence of how the organization works and how people in the organization interact, learning and adapting to changing circumstances.

The Agency for Healthcare Research and Quality is a government agency that sponsors a project called the "Learning Health System."[16] The project centers around how healthcare organizations use internal data and external evidence to improve their operations and care processes. Just like a human brain learns from internal and external experiences, the Learning Health System is adaptive and flexible, learning and evolving over time.

We should care that the health IT stack is diverse, dynamic, and flexible. When an organization aspires for clinicians to give the best care and for patients to receive it, the IT environment needs to adjust and learn and adapt. A flexible, modular, and adaptive IT stack allows the organization to learn faster than a monolithic, one-size-fits-all, single-vendor system.

I look at a health system the way a neurologist might check for optimal brain function—fast reaction times, excellent coordination and agility, and constantly learning. Learning is iterative. We learn by trying new approaches. Sometimes they work, and sometimes they don't. The human brain and the modern health system learn by trial and error, iteratively improving their performance.

---

16   Agency for Healthcare Research and Quality, "About Learning Health Systems," March 2019, https://www.ahrq.gov/learning-health-systems/about.html.

CHAPTER 2

HEALTHCARE'S CHANGING LANDSCAPE

In the 1990s and early 2000s, hospitals started buying primary care physician (PCP) practices. This led to the formation of "health systems"—organizations consisting of one or more hospitals with a variety of specialty practices and primary care offices spread out in a region around the hospitals. These PCPs were to be "feeders," meant to refer patients to the specialists and hospitals within the system.

Things have changed, and today it's health plan owners and insurance companies that are buying the PCP practices. The largest employer of physicians today is UnitedHealth Group under their Optum brand. Humana owns and operates physician practices under their CenterWell and Conviva Care Solutions brands. Aetna CVS Health operates Minute Clinics inside their CVS stores, and also purchased Oak Street Health, a group of primary care practices focused on primary care practices in underserved areas.

The new role of the PCP is not to feed patients toward the specialists and hospitals, but rather as first line of defense, aiming to keep patients healthy, manage chronic conditions, and avoid acute care utilization as much as possible. By managing the patient at the primary care level, the practice avoids expensive ED visits and hospitalizations.

The US healthcare system is always in a state of flux. If you work for a healthcare organization, you're in a permanent state of transition, and you're always in practice transformation mode. I look at change from three angles: reimbursement models, care models, and technology models. Obviously, these three circles overlap like a Venn diagram, which is exactly why all three circles need to be able to move and change together.

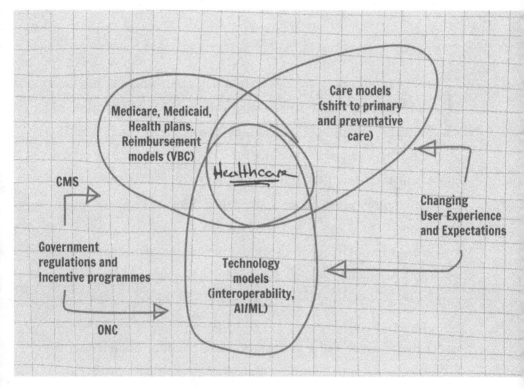

Figure 2: Factors driving change in healthcare

To see this at work, let's walk into an Oak Street Health or ChenMed practice. These practices focus on Medicare Advantage contracts where they receive a per-member-per-month payment[17] for every enrolled patient. Under this payment model, the team will provide care for each patient in the practice, with the goal of keeping them healthy and avoiding acute care as much as possible. The first thing to notice is the team: there is a doctor, a medical assistant, and a nurse, and also social workers, community workers, behavioral health professionals (either in person on-site, or available via telehealth link), and a care coordinator. Together, the team works with the patient to help them stay healthy, monitoring medical conditions and needs and addressing housing, food security, and support by family or other caregivers. The team's goal is to keep the patient healthy, and living at home, and to prevent expensive visits to the ED or the hospital.

In addition to having an expanded care team with a variety of functions and skills, these VBC practices track their patients differently. In the traditional model, patients make an appointment to see the doctor. The doctor sees anyone who schedules a visit and shows up in the waiting room. A patient who doesn't schedule a visit is off the radar in most traditional practices. However, in a VBC model, the practice tracks all patients under their care—what we call their "population" or "panel." This requires population health management software, either as an additional feature of the existing EHR or as a separate software component. The population health management system shows the providers who their patients are, which ones have certain chronic conditions, and those most likely to need assistance. The care team uses this software to provide proactive care and reach out to the patient directly, preventing a visit to the ED.

---

17   "How Oak Street Health's Value-Based Care Structure Is Bolstering Healthy Equity in Underserved Communities," February 15, 2022, https://www.oakstreethealth.com/osh-value-based-care-751584.

Besides the population health management module in the practice EHR, there are other technologies to help the team manage and track the care for their patient panel. Modern diagnostic tools—such as point-of-care ultrasound systems, and smart stethoscopes—allow the practice team to diagnose problems on the spot. In the past they referred the patient to an off-site imaging center or cardiology practice. Telehealth modules within the practice allow the team to bring in behavioral health or other specialty experts while the patient is in the office. These new technologies, both in the IT space as well as in the connected device space, shift the care model away from specialty care toward the primary care team, lowering the overall cost of the care. The VBC model also connects the patient to community-based organizations (CBOs) to provide food, transportation, utility assistance, benefits coordination, and other services that help patients manage their health and their lives.

In this example of a practice running on VBC contracts, you see the three drivers at work:

- Reimbursement model: New contracts create an opportunity to redefine how the practice works.

- Care model: An expanded team with skill sets not found in a traditional practice, providing the patient with efficient and team-based care. Care coordination and teamwork are important elements in the new care model.

- Technologies: Information tools and connected devices, communication tools connecting the practice to outside organizations, all working together to support the new care model. The technology stack in this practice is not limited to the standard EHR and billing system, and it includes connections to other devices and other organizational networks.

Let's look at each of these drivers in more detail.

Reimbursement Models

"Form follows finance," says Dr. Dan Martich, chief health informatics officer at Trinity Health, putting a twist on the "form follows function" adage. He is correct: in healthcare, just like in most other industries, the funding mechanisms determine how the work is done and how the product or service is delivered. As the payment rules change, so does the workflow.

US healthcare payment models have gradually transitioned from fee-for-service to reimbursement tied to quality and value.

> Health IT is really the neurology of the organization. Health information systems determine how the organization works, how team members communicate, and how patients interact with the organization.

The collective term is "value-based care," or population health, inside of which exists a variety of payment models, each with a different set of incentives, different metrics, different patients, and different providers.

While the traditional fee-for-service models using a predetermined fee schedule are relatively straightforward, the new VBC reimbursement models are more complicated. A healthcare provider may have contracts with multiple health plans, each with different incentive rules, based on quality or utilization measures, comparisons to benchmarks, or some form of capitation, a fixed per-member-permonth fee for each patient under their care. This all adds complexity in billing and reimbursement, and care delivery.

Healthcare providers need to reassess their position during the reimbursement transition by asking the following questions:

- Have we optimized our payments according to the mix of payment plans?

- Are our providers aware of the incentives and disincentives for each of their patients, and are they able to act in both the patient's best interests but also the organization's bottom line?

- What metrics do we need to track (retrospectively) and predict (prospectively) our business model versus our payer mix?

- Do we need to adjust our product lines or service lines to optimize reimbursement? More care management? More or less long-term care? Invest or divest urgent care? More cardiology or more palliative care?

Assessing the bottom line was easier in the fee-for-service world, as the rule was *more is better*. Under the VBC payments, that's not always the case, as the rules keep changing.

Care Models

As payment models evolve, healthcare providers need to adjust care models to align incentives and maintain an operating margin. In the old fee-for-service, more-is-better model, volume was the primary metric for success: more admissions, more procedures, more ED visits. But with fee-for-service being transitioned to VBC reimbursement, the care models change.

The shift in reimbursement structure drives the following changes in the care model:

- The focus shifts from preventable acute care to ambulatory and preventive care.

- Care management and care coordination teams are introduced. These teams didn't exist ten years ago, and now almost every organization, large or small, employs care coordinators precisely to avoid acute care, and to optimize quality measures—in other words to align the care model with the reimbursement model.

- The new reimbursement models have altered the competitive landscape and introduced new players, specifically built to maximize operating margins under the new rules: Accountable Care Organizations (ACOs), ACO Realizing Equity, Access, and Community Health (ACO REACH) practices, and practice groups with at-risk Medicare Advantage contracts. These new players require a change in your care model, to help you reclaim revenue that would otherwise flow to them.

- Taking care of a challenging population may require organizations to strengthen behavioral health services, community support services, food or housing support, and other service lines that would not be part of the "traditional" healthcare organization.

- Shifting care from the hospital to the home. Using at-home devices and remote patient monitoring is a technology play, but it's also a change in the care model that transitions patients from the hospital setting to their home.

There are many other ways to change how we care for patients. This is an area of rapid innovation driven by consumer preferences and competitive pressures. Innovative healthcare organizations enable providers to offer their patients in-home services such as hospice, telehealth access, housing assistance, transportation, health education, or nutrition; supervised in-home care; and any other combination of care tailored to the patient and cost-effective to the organization.

Technology Models

Technology options change even faster than reimbursement models and care models. The healthcare industry is often slow on the uptake and scaling of new technologies. Unvendoring should speed up the introduction and application of new technologies.

New technologies clearly enable new methods for caring for patients in the home and other nontraditional settings:

- Hospital-at-home and hospital-to-home—using in-home monitors, high-speed communication and data exchange, low-cost devices, and the ability to connect care providers to the patient and care team in the patient's home.

- Patient and family engagement apps create another pathway to connect to the patient's care team.

New technologies also introduce innovative options inside the organization. Many of these come from outside the healthcare industry but can have a significant impact on care delivery and efficiency inside the organization. We'll look at these in more detail in a later chapter. For example:

- Innovative clinical documentation tools. Care providers spend significant time managing clinical documentation, and new AI technologies can help make this faster, more efficient, and less burdensome for clinicians. Many clinicians use this tech today, but there is ample opportunity to do more, with a greater variety of tools, for many clinicians today who simply click boxes on templates. Speech to text, ambient clinical documentation (doctor-patient exam room conversation recorded and converted to a visit note), and documentation bots all need to find their way into care providers' toolkits.

- RPA is a range of tools and technologies designed to automate and speed up processes inside the organization: transportation, delivery, ordering and fulfillment, customer service, meal preparation and delivery, and room availability and turnaround. A hospital is a tangle of processes, and the opportunities for process automation are endless.

- Decision Support (DS), AI, and ML. We will look at these in more detail in chapter 8. The combination of DS/ML/AI has two levels: the patient level and the organizational level. Both offer great potential for technology adoption. At the patient level, DS tools can help provide the right care at the right time. The clinical DS movement has promised this for years, but it needs more attention. There is great opportunity for DS/ML/AI at the organization level: What strategic organizational decisions need to be made to deliver better care to more people at lower cost? Which care management strategies work? Which patient populations can we address better? How do we optimize payer contracts? How do we ensure we meet contract incentives for the various plans? As Figure 3 illustrates, there are many concurrent VBC contracts in place, with care provided by multiple providers in multiple settings. How can we maximize the quality of our care and our reimbursement at the same time? Organizational decision-making is complex and driven by many inputs and will require advanced DS/ML/AI tools to find the best strategy for our organization—today, tomorrow, and into the future.

Whether it's a new payment model, new connectivity to in-home devices, or new DS or analytics models, the large megavendors will get there, but they will be several years late. In the meantime, third-party companies can move faster, innovate faster, and have solutions available well before the megavendor.

The advantages of moving early with third-party technologies are that your organization will learn to operate faster with the new payment model, care model, or technology model. A greater diversity of technologies and solutions is the shot in the arm every organization needs for IT agility and learning adaptation.

The introduction of population health and VBC around 2014 illustrates the third-party effect. KLAS Research published their first report on population health trends, the "Population Health 2014 Perception" report.[18] The summary conclusion was: Population health is new, it's up and coming, and it will offer competitive advantages to organizations who implement these programs early. The key recommendations were:

- Select a population health management system now, from one of a variety of up-and-coming IT firms.

- Don't sign long-term contracts. Sign a short-term contract and plan to replace the system in a few years, once the market has more experiences with the requirements of population health.

---

18   Mark Allphin, "Population Health 2014 Perception,"
      KLAS Research, 2014, https://klasresearch.com/report/
      population-health-2014-perception-who-are-providers-betting-on/907.

- Learn from the early adoption experience and apply that learning to your longer-term strategy.

- Don't wait for your large EHR vendor to implement population health management, as you will lose competitive advantage to early movers.

Nearly ten years on from the KLAS report, many healthcare organizations have implemented population health management systems, covering analytics, risk stratification, care coordination, and patient engagement tools. Some of the EHR megavendors now offer these capabilities inside their EHR suites, but their functionality hasn't matched advanced specialized firms. In the competitive and fast-moving population health/VBC space, unvendoring would have paid off ten years ago.

The population health/VBC example also illustrates the key premise of this chapter: how reimbursement changes gave birth to new care models, which rely on implementing and executing new technologies. These three drivers are always on the move, constantly shifting the ground on which we are building. Be agile.

Changing User Experience and Expectations

As healthcare organizations change, there is a parallel change underway in the way people interact with healthcare organizations. The people on the inside—the workers and team members—as well as the clients, customers, and patients, change the way they work and communicate. This, too, requires that we respond rapidly to change.

For example, healthcare workers perform as teams of physicians, nurses, therapists, pharmacists, social workers, and care coordinators, each playing a specific role in the care for the patient. Each patient is a "project" with specific tasks and dependencies. In most industries, teams use collaboration software such as Slack to help them manage their projects, coordinate their tasks, and communicate in a succinct and efficient manner. The typical EHR is a record, which controls everything that happens in the hospital, but it's often lacking in facilitating the collaboration around the care of a patient. Most EHRs do not have a Slack-like built-in function. The teamwork experience in a healthcare setting is very different from for a software engineering team.

Many patients today live in the digital world and have modern expectations from their healthcare providers. Luckily, all EHRs today have a patient-facing portal (thanks to the Meaningful Use requirements stipulating electronic patient access starting in 2015[19]), and most EHRs have a phone app for patients. However, these portals and apps are extensions of the provider's EHR, and you may have to use one portal or app in your dealings with a hospital and a specialist doctor, and an entirely different patient setup and app for your primary care doctor. Today, there is no single healthcare app where a patient can work with all their doctors and healthcare providers using an app of their choice. They are "tethered" to the providers' EHRs.

Compare this to buying a plane ticket: A customer can order plane tickets from United Airlines and American Airlines through their specific websites. The same customer can also order tickets on any airline from Kayak or Expedia, including hotel stays and car rentals too. Consumers purchasing travel are not tethered to each airline's specific system; they can choose the platform they are most

---

19   S. E. Waldren and E. Solis, "The Evolution of Meaningful Use: Today, Stage 3, and Beyond," *Family Practice Management* 23, no. 1 (January–February 2016): 17–22, PMID: 26761299.

familiar with. That's not how we interact with healthcare providers today.

The expectations and experiences of tech users also change, impacting both staff and patients. This is not a threat to operations but an opportunity to embrace the future and bring the IT team along for the ride.

Government Regulations Pushing for Change

The US government plays an important role in driving and directing the change in healthcare models. This happens in two ways: the Centers for Medicare and Medicaid Services (CMS) is leveraging the reimbursement model to drive change. The Office of the National Coordinator for Health Information Technology (ONC) is setting standards and requirements for EHR firms and is using the technology model as its change agent. Together, in coordination with each other, they set the future of health policy.

Mark Scrimshire, chief interoperability officer at Onyx Healthcare stated, "ONC is more about the provider community, and CMS is more about the payers. ONC is pushing on the certifications of EHRs and the need to support application program interfaces (APIs) for data exchange. That lays the groundwork for CMS to require payers to share more data with providers so they can get into VBC relationships with them and share information." This shows the interplay between reimbursement, technology, and care model.

Scrimshire also points out how government initiatives trump return on investment (ROI) discussions: "Compliance is non-discretionary, it's money that must be spent. You might talk about ROI, but compliance is a different budget line. I'm not going to be noncompliant with CMS, I need to check that box." Compliance jumps to the top of the to-do list.

Aneesh Chopra, former White House chief technology officer, tells it from a health system CIO perspective: "CIOs are caught between success under the CMS rule and success under the ONC rules. And they are caught between enabling EHR vendor features and being the advocate partner to the users, to make sure that what they need gets done."

We can connect the dots, from the Meaningful Use program to EHR adoption at health systems and practices, to prepare the IT infrastructure for VBC and alternative payment and care models. It was a deliberate and industry-changing set of government regulatory actions that got us to where we are today.

Workbook

In this workbook section, we'll explore two examples of the changing reimbursement environment: the care model and the technology options. As you work through these examples, keep the "form follows finance" mantra in mind. As in all other organizations and business scenarios, follow the money.

PAYERS AND PROVIDERS BECOMING "PAYVIDERS"

Figure 3 shows how alternative payment models (APMs) change over time. I encourage you to download and read the related Health Care Payment Learning and Action Network APM white paper.[20] Figure 3 shows the evolution of payment models. Category 1 is fee-for-service healthcare, which significantly diminished in the future

---

20   Mitre Corporation, "APM Framework," 2017, https://hcp-lan.org/workproducts/apm-refresh-whitepaper-final.pdf.

state. Categories 2, 3, and 4 are versions of APMs that incrementally shift the financial risk from the payer to the provider. Moving toward the right side of the chart, the provider organization takes on more and more aspects of the payer role, leading to the "payvider" portmanteau.[21] Category 2 and 3 payment plans give providers financial incentives for improved quality and reduced utilization. Category 4 is based on fixed population-based payments, per member per month, which shifts the financial upside and downside entirely to the provider organization (with exceptions and stop-loss provisions for catastrophic cases).

---

21 Zachary N. Goldberg and David B. Nash, "The Payvider: An Evolving Model," *College of Population Health Faculty Papers*, Paper 134 (2021), https://jdc.jefferson.edu/healthpolicyfaculty/134.

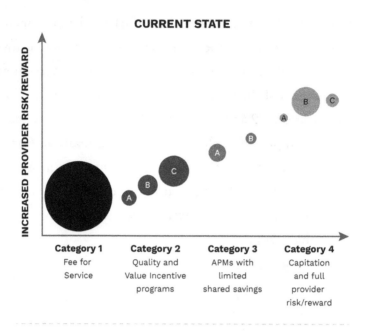

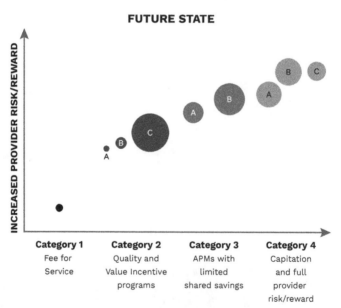

Figure 3: APMs in current and future state (source: Health Care Payment Learning and Action Network)[22]

---

22   Mitre Corporation, "APM Framework," https://hcp-lan.org/workproducts/apm-refresh-whitepaper-final.pdf.

The arrow on the left shows some of the changes that occur when a practice transitions toward the right and more VBC, higher accountability, and innovation. There are financial incentives for quality and utilization and better organizational integration and team coordination. This trend impacts how we deliver care and how we work as a team, all of which require IT support.

Ask yourself these questions as you study the diagram of current and future state:

- Where is your organization today? First picture? Second picture? Somewhere in between?

- Where do you see your organization headed? Do you see a movement toward the future state in your patient base, and in your provider base?

- What does that mean for your information systems and how providers and caregivers work?

One more thought on these diagrams: In the current state, there is one predominant reimbursement system—fee-for-service. In the future state, it seems that there may not be one single reimbursement system but rather a mix of reimbursement models concurrently dependent on the patient's health plan. This creates a very complex situation. What should you do? How are you incentivized for this patient? How do your providers and caregivers take the reimbursement model into account as they care for their patients? How do you manage this complexity?

The answer is sophisticated health IT on a diverse and dynamic set of applications in your stack.

ELECTRONIC HEALTH RECORD OR POPULATION MANAGEMENT SYSTEM?

Is your EHR optimized to work in a fee-for-service environment? Does it support your VBC method of practice? Let's ask a few questions to see in which direction your clinical infrastructure leans.

Table 2. Comparing care models under fee-for-service and VBC payment plans

	MORE FEE-FOR-SERVICE ORIENTED	MORE POPULATION HEALTH FOCUSED
PATIENT LIST	I see my patient schedule for the day.	I see today's patient schedule but also a list of patients who I may need to call or reach out to.
TEAMWORK	I perform my tasks—my notes, my orders.	The system lets each team member do their tasks—clinical, social work, behavioral health—and I can see an overview of everyone's tasks.
REFERRALS	I can refer to specialists.	I can refer to specialists but also to local food pantries, housing support, benefits coordination, family support, and other community services.
ACCESS TO OUTSIDE PATIENT DATA	I mostly see clinical data from within my practice. I get discharge letters from the ED and hospital directly into my EHR.	I see data from within my practice but also from other healthcare organizations. I get real-time alerts if one of my patients checks into a hospital or emergency room in the area, so I can reach out and potentially avoid a hospitalization.
CONNECTION TO PATIENT'S HOME AND FAMILY	The patient's family can use the portal to see the patient's healthcare data.	I get updates from the patient's home devices (blood pressure, weight, daily activity), and the patient's family is able to message directly to the care team.
POSTACUTE CARE	I do not have access to data from patients in a nursing home or assisted living facility.	My team can view clinical data, medications, and nurses' notes for any patients in a postacute care facility.

If you checked one or more boxes on the right side, which is more focused on support for population health, do those features come directly from your EHR, or should you use separate software components? What would optimize the workflow for your team?

Now that you have put your organization somewhere on the single-vendor/diverse stack continuum, let's build a case for why a diverse environment is better for the organization, better for patients and clinicians—and more futureproof.

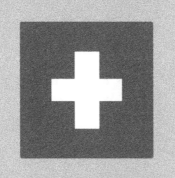

CHAPTER 3

THE CASE FOR A DIVERSE HEALTH IT STACK

Mini Case Study 1

Imagine a hospital with a strong single-vendor mindset. A nearby large primary care practice and a clinic run by the Veterans Health Administration send patients to the ED in this regional hospital. The ED physicians require more specific, complete, and up-to-date information about these referred patients—a brief medical background and a reason for the referral. The ED physician can call the referring physician by phone but typically gets a lengthy and inefficient conversation. They would much prefer a short, concise document.

The industry standard approach is to send an electronic referral to the ED, using Direct Secure Messaging, a recognized Health Insurance Portability and Accountability Act (HIPAA)-compliant messaging method. The referral message includes an attachment with the medical history and reason for referral.

Now comes the problem.

The ED also gets referrals from practices that are on the same EHR as the ED. These referrals go through the vendor's proprietary channels. Now the ED team has to monitor two inboxes: one from same-EHR practices and a different one from other-EHR practices. To avoid this two-list situation, the hospital asks the referring practices not to use Direct Messaging from their own EHR, but rather log on to the hospital's EHR portal and enter the referral there.

It's old-school single-vendor thinking competing with outside-the-EHR-box thinking.

Old-school: The hospital wants their staff to monitor only one referral list to make sure they force their referring practices to step outside their EHRs into the hospital portal. Less work for us, more work for you.

Outside-the-EHR-box: Use Direct Messaging, the current industry standard available for communicating referrals (and discharges and other patient-related communication). We want to be *agile*, allowing other practices to adopt electronic referrals without a lot of effort. We want to be *competitive and encourage business growth* by making it attractive to other practices to send us their patients. We want to be *efficient*, replacing long phone calls with concise medical documents. Finally, we want to be *clinician-friendly* by offering both the referring physician and the ED team an effective and efficient method for handing off referrals.

Mini Case Study 2

Let's look at another single-vendor mindset example. A teaching hospital has a large residency program and a hospitalist service, together managing a significant number of their inpatients. Every day has a large number of admissions and discharges. Resident teams and hospitalists switch in and out, depending on their shifts. The teams spend a lot of time coordinating the care for their patients, assigning patients to teams, updating each other on next steps and action plans for each patient. The tool they use: printed copies of Excel spreadsheets, updated twice a day.

The residency program approached CareAlign, a team communication and coordination platform, similar to Slack for software engineers working on complex projects (see chapter 7). CareAlign is connected to the EHR: clinical data goes from the EHR to CareAlign, and notes and updates flow from CareAlign to the EHR.

After several demonstrations and discussions with both the clinical and IT teams, the hospital decided to not pursue the third-party team tool. Pricing may have been a concern, although the CareAlign tool has a good ROI record. The single-vendor mindset was an obstacle: the organization feels that putting a separate user interface layer and team communication tool on top of the EHR would detract from clinical work.

Old school: users should be in a single system, and having clinical teams using the EHR and the team communication system simultaneously would cause confusion. Let's remember that a paper printout is also a separate system with a separate user interface.

Outside the EHR box: EHRs are best in single-patient single-user situations. It's not the best tool for team communication and coordination on a panel of patients. A third-party module, integrated with the EHR for exchange of key data elements, can make the workflow faster and *more efficient.* It can *improve the clinician experience* from working on printed sheets to the clinical version of Slack. And by making the care process more efficient, especially for admissions and discharges, it makes the hospital more fiscally sound and competitive.

The four reasons build the case for moving toward a diverse, multiplayer health IT environment: agility and innovation, competitiveness and business growth, efficiency and cost reduction, and clinician friendliness.

What Is the Stack?

"Stack" is IT-speak for the various technologies that power an organization's business processes. These technologies are often shown in a diagram as a stack of layers, with the fundamental data sources at the bottom, data integration layers and application layers in the middle, and user-interface layers at the top. An organization's IT stack can include analytics modules, AI and ML components, interoperability layers, and a wide variety of data input systems.

Before we jump in, I need to make the clarification that we're talking about the application stack or software stack, not the technology stack. The technology stack covers not only software but also the hardware platform, networking, firewalls, databases, back-end tools, and more. For this book, "stack" applies to application stack, the set of applications and software components that run the healthcare organization.

Here is my representation of a typical health IT stack for a large health system with inpatient facilities and ambulatory practices.[23] The main layers of the stack start with the data sources at the foundation layers, interoperability, data exchange, and analytics on top of the

23   Becoming a Data Scientist, "Choosing a Data Science Technology Stack [w/ Survey]," July 26, 2013, https://becomingadatascientist.wordpress.com/2013/07/26/choosing-a-data-science-technology-stack-w-survey/; Jan-Felix Schneider, "Value-Based Care Stack Part II," *Health Tech Stack* (blog), June 23, 2022, https://www.healthtechstack.io/p/value-based-care-stack-part-ii.

data, then a large layer of clinical and operational applications. The top layer has patient- and provider-facing tools and applications.

Patient Engagement		Provider Engagement	
Connected Apps • Portals • RPM / PERS • Telehealth		EHR • Provider Portals • Referrals • Connected Apps	

Clin Care / Operations		Business Functions	
Emergency Dept • Referrals • EHR Acute • eRx • Care Coordination • AI modules • EHR Ambulatory • Behavioral Health • External Data Exch • Medications / Rx • Nursing Applications • RPA • Diagnostic Depts – Lab • Clin. Decision Support • Rad, GI, Card etc. • Clinical Documentation • Scheduling		HR • Contracting • Legal / ROI • Insurance • Rev Cycle / CRM • RPA • HIM/Coding	

Analytics	Data Mgmt	Data Exchange
Pop Health • Research • BI • Clin/Operational • AI/ML • Precision Med • Visualization	Risk Strat • Aggregation/ETL • Enterprise DWH	HIE / QHIN • RPM • National Exchange • Home Health • Telehealth • CBO referrals • Post-Acute

Inputs / Data Sources
EHR • Claims Files – Rev Cycle • HIE / Outside Data • Dept System • SDoH • Diagnostic Devices • CRM • Clin Documentation • RPM devices

Figure 4: Health IT stack for large health system

A best-of-breed organization will have stack components from many different vendors, and as data moves up the stack through presentation and processing layers, it passes from one company's system to another. On the other end of the spectrum, a single-vendor health organization's stack consists of layers all from the same firm. Healthcare megavendors provide the organization's full stack, all from one firm, which allows all layers to communicate effectively with the other layers (supposedly), and for data to flow smoothly from bottom (source) to top (users).

Bringing Diversity into the Health IT Stack

From this point, the pendulum swings back toward best of breed but in a different configuration: the core of the stack is dominated by layers from one vendor, which we'll call the "platform." Health organizations can now supplement this platform stack with components and modules from efficient third-party fast-innovation firms, moving from a single-vendor stack toward a more diverse and agile IT stack.

A stack consisting of a single-vendor platform with one or more add-on modules is made possible by the introduction and implementation of APIs based on the FHIR standard (see chapter 6). The 21st Century Cures Act requires EHR vendors to support FHIR-based APIs in order to receive certification. These APIs allow other systems and modules to connect and share data. APIs enable health systems to create a more diverse stack (components from a variety of vendors) and a more agile stack (switching out components without having to replace the entire stack or a layer in the stack). A more diverse and agile stack is critical to support the healthcare team in the fast-changing healthcare environment.

Building and maintaining a diverse health IT stack should be based on a solid business foundation. The case for a diverse and agile stack rests on the following four pillars: agility and innovation, growth and competitiveness, cost reduction, and clinician well-being.

Agility and Innovation

Every action, transaction, and interaction in healthcare is powered by an information system. Think about a physician's daily tasks in any healthcare setting, whether it's a large hospital or a small practice:

every test, medication, appointment, clinical decision, or communication to a team member requires entering the data into the EHR. A simple verbal communication between two clinicians ("Let's check her liver functions and then start medication treatment.") immediately becomes a lab order, a medication prescription, and a line in the assessment and plan section of the EHR clinical note.

As discussed in chapter 2, healthcare changes fast. Every change in the way we deliver healthcare requires a corresponding change in our IT. VBC requires care coordination systems, digital patient engagement, analytics, and risk stratification. Without these, the organization cannot support care delivery in a VBC setting. We either wait and hope for VBC support from our single-vendor stack or include one or several modules from fast-moving technology firms.

A diverse health IT stack enables rapid implementation of new technologies to support new payment and care models, new interoperability and data exchange, and new technology components. It also supports a learn-fast/fail-fast approach, which was advocated in the KLAS perception report on population health: don't sign long-term contracts, but rather invest in new technologies with a short time horizon, leading to a quick win or a fast failure.

I asked Dr. Rasu Shrestha, chief innovation and commercialization officer at Advocate Health in North Carolina, if he sees a diverse IT stack as a path to innovation. He says: "I think it's one of several ingredients. I think having a singular vendor stack impedes innovation. Is the converse true? It is an ingredient, it's a core ingredient. But having a diverse IT stack onto itself doesn't equate to ability to excel in innovation. The health IT vendor would say they are creating an ecosystem allowing for innovation, but the reality is that a singular vendor impedes innovation. A diverse stack is one of several essential ingredients to allow for transformative leaps forward."

Competitiveness and Business Growth

Healthcare is not only changing fast, but also becoming competitive at many levels. Competition is not just between various health systems in the area. Large insurance firms buy healthcare providers or partner with healthcare providers. UnitedHealth Group's Optum subsidiary is now the largest employer of physicians in the US, with more than 90,000 physicians and 2,200 practices. CVS and Humana also own many physician practices.[24] New practices funded by venture capital funds move into your region and compete with your practices. Oak Street Health is expanding to additional states[25] and Amazon-owned One Medical is opening new practices in new US markets.[26]

VBC primary care practices such as Oak Street Health and ChenMed are another example of the need to compete with technology and innovation. These practices advertise heavily with team-based care—a focus on keeping patients healthy and out of the hospital, a focus on wellness for seniors, and a strong commitment to community. They recruit new patients and move them into a Medicare Advantage contract with full capitation. They use advanced information tools to risk-stratify the patient population, which sharply reduces the need for ED visits and hospitalizations in this population. Our health-system-owned traditional practice sees patients leave and move to

24   R. Hatton, "The Groups Dominating Physician Employment," Physician Leadership, March 2024, https://www.beckersphysicianleadership.com/physician-workforce/the-groups-dominating-physician-employment.html.

25   Heather Landi, "Oak Street Health Unveils Expansion Plans to Open Centers in 4 New States," June 1, 2023, www.fiercehealthcare.com/providers/oak-street-health-unveils-expansion-plans-4-new-states.

26   Bruce Japsen, "A Year After Amazon Purchase, One Medical Adds Clinics and New Markets," Forbes, April 8, 2024, https://www.forbes.com/sites/brucejapsen/2024/04/05/year-after-amazon-purchase-one-medical-adds-clinics-and-new-markets/.

Oak Street. They may also see some of the providers move because the VBC organizations pay their PCPs well.

In order to compete with the new reality, these health systems need to match and exceed the new model of care: advertise, participate in VBC contracts, enroll patients in risk-based insurance plans, and create a large enough patient population to make capitation work. They need a software solution to monitor the population, coordinate care, and track the utilization and spending on the attributed patient population. The EHR vendor may not provide this, but by adding a population health management component to the stack, they can beat the competitor at their own game. To succeed, they must adapt to the new competitive business reality, adopt a new workflow, and implement new technologies to keep the practice competitive with emerging competitors and emerging care models.

Cost Reduction

Single-vendor EHRs are extremely expensive. This is not the place for an exact price comparison. The vendors and providers keep the numbers secret, but the cost of implementation and operations of an EHR system range from tens of millions to hundreds of millions, with the high end being the Partners Health Epic implementation at more than $1 billion.[27]

If your organization has contracted for a single-vendor EHR recently, it's apparent that there is very little room for negotiation. The argument goes, from the vendor's perspective: we charge all our clients the same; it wouldn't be fair if we give you a better deal than our other

---

27   Naomi Diaz, "5 Systems Spend Millions on EHR Installs," January 2023, https://www.beckershospitalreview.com/ehrs/most-expensive-ehr-installs.html; Gabriel Perna, "How Epic Took Over the Hospital EHR Market," September 18, 2023, https://www.modernhealthcare.com/digital-health/epic-cerner-meditech-ehr-market.

vendors, so here is the standard best pricing that's based on the exact same pricing model for all our other clients. Take it or leave it.

Big vendors' "enterprise license" strategies initially seem like a good deal for the health system, but in the long run they turn out to be a financial trap, as we'll see in chapter 4. Once your organization has paid for the all-in contract, it seems wasteful and excessive to purchase add-ons from other vendors. The CEO and CFO will question why add-ons weren't included in the main vendor contract.

While today it may be hard to make the case that unvendoring reduces your total IT spending, I see it as the only way out of the single-vendor contract trap. You can start to include replacement modules such as a third-party analytics suite or a third-party department system. Now you're able to negotiate to exclude these modules from the contract. It's not easy to go à la carte at an all-you-can-eat restaurant, but you need to start by putting yourself in the position to turn down the all-in price. You'll lose weight too.

Clinician Well-Being

Proponents of large-vendor EHRs explain that a single, uniform, standardized user interface or UX benefits the users: once they learn how the system works, and since it's the same for all locations and all employees, users can easily move around to other departments, other teams, or other roles without having to relearn a new system. Also, users can easily help each other since the system is the same for everyone. In my role as a large health system CMIO, I used to see this as a benefit, and almost as a best practice for clinical IT: UX uniformity and standardization for greater organizational efficiency.

No more. We have moved beyond that point, in several ways.

Users are different, with different work styles, different preferences, and different methods of efficiency. Some doctors and nurses type faster than they talk. Others are great at documentation via dictation and speech-to-text. Some providers are becoming great at ambient clinical documentation.[28] Some providers use the computers in the clinic or the hospital unit, while others use their phones or other mobile devices. There are many innovative technologies available today that enrich the UX and add value to the overall health IT stack.

EHR time/motion research shows that physicians and providers spend about half (!) of their time on clinical documentation.[29] That isn't acceptable from anyone's perspective. It's wasteful of our clinicians' time, of healthcare dollars, and of patients' experience in interacting with their providers. There are many tools, devices, and apps that make clinicians more efficient and reduce the amount of time working on the EHR. Each of these technologies deserves a spot in your organization's stack (or at least as a trial). We will look at these add-on technologies in more detail in chapter 7.

The final reason to move past the single UX argument is that most users today have grown up in digital environments. People are used to doing things quickly, easily, and naturally. Speak to your phone, swipe to an app, take a picture, and connect with another device—that's how we work. We have moved past the need to have everyone use the exact same tools to do their work. We live in a much more diverse and agile technology environment that can also thrive inside a healthcare organization.

---

28 "Ambient documentation" means having a microphone in the room where provider and patient speak and using the conversation between patient and provider as input to the provider's clinical note.

29 C. Sinsky et al., "Allocation of Physician Time in Ambulatory Practice: A Time and Motion Study in 4 Specialties," *Annals of Internal Medicine* 165, no. 11 (December 6, 2016): 753–60, https://doi.org/10.7326/M16-0961, EPUB September 6, 2016, PMID: 27595430.

In fact, the case for a diverse healthcare stack parallels the case for diversity in the environment, in society, and in the workplace. A diverse health IT stack is more adaptable to change and allows your organization to act and react faster to changing competitive needs. It also allows you to negotiate with, and create independence from, your large EHR vendor. This creates opportunities for many experiments in efficiency and user-friendliness. The benefits far outweigh the risks.

The market is shifting from single vendor to a new version of best of breed, the diverse health IT stack. We can help by giving a little push in the right direction. Be the change agent. If you see your organization behaving with a single-vendor, inwardly focused mindset, challenge it by offering out-of-the-EHR-box solutions. Add applications to the EHR and turn on any feature that makes your organization easier to do business with—for healthcare partners, for patients, and for your own clinical team.

Data Security

While we argue the case in favor of a diverse IT stack, we also should confront the most common argument against including multiple applications in the stack: data security. Healthcare data is private and can be sensitive. Healthcare providers are a prime target for hackers, phishing attempts, and ransomware attacks. Data breaches are costly both in terms of financial penalties and in loss of reputation and trust. Fewer applications and vendors in the stack means fewer points of entry for troublemakers.

I am no expert on data security, so I won't go into details on balancing the threat of data breaches with the business need. However, health systems have a chief information security officer or equivalent who is in charge of keeping systems secure, preventing breaches, and keeping staff on the alert for potential compromises to the organization's data privacy. They are your support to define conditions and precautions on data-secure implementation of third-party software. Just saying "no" to third-party applications or software from start-up vendors is not the only way or the best way to protect data.

Relying on one vendor for the sake of security can also backfire as a single point of failure with all eggs in the same basket. Obviously, all healthcare organizations have backup mechanisms, redundancies, and downtime procedures. Some third-party applications (chapter 7) may serve as partial data backup or as a downtime solution. Sure, redundancy could be a backup data server in a bunker in Arizona, but you can also get redundancy from your care coordination or team communication software keeping the team up to date during an EHR outage.

Workbook

This chapter's workbook features two stack-related problem sets. First, I would like you to think through the applications in your organization's stack: Do they come primarily from the same vendor, or do you have several different IT vendors represented in your IT stack? The second topic will look at the cost and ROI for health IT projects, as the lead-in to the following chapter.

HOW DIVERSE OR MONOLITHIC IS YOUR ORGANIZATION'S APPLICATION STACK?

Here is a stack diagram for a single-vendor dominant stack. All items in bold are from the same health IT vendor. Many health systems today have a stack that resembles this picture. The crossed-out modules are not implemented at this organization. This single-vendor diagram represents a health system with acute and ambulatory facilities. By removing a few of the inpatient-specific functions, the same diagram represents an ambulatory-only organization.

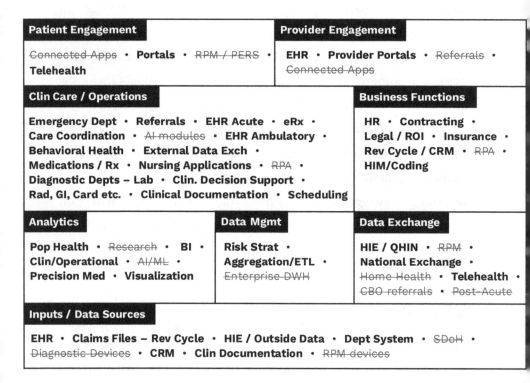

Figure 5: Single-vendor dominated health IT stack

In this next stack diagram, circle the modules from the main health IT vendor in use in your organization. Cross out any applications not in use. Use a different color to mark modules from a different vendor. You can mark the vendor for these modules in the margin.

Patient Engagement		Provider Engagement	
Connected Apps • Portals • RPM / PERS • Telehealth		EHR • Provider Portals • Referrals • Connected Apps	

Clin Care / Operations		Business Functions	
Emergency Dept • Referrals • EHR Acute • eRx • Care Coordination • AI modules • EHR Ambulatory • Behavioral Health • External Data Exch • Medications / Rx • Nursing Applications • RPA • Diagnostic Depts – Lab • Clin. Decision Support • Rad, GI, Card etc. • Clinical Documentation • Scheduling		HR • Contracting • Legal / ROI • Insurance • Rev Cycle / CRM • RPA • HIM/Coding	

Analytics	Data Mgmt	Data Exchange
Pop Health • Research • BI • Clin/Operational • AI/ML • Precision Med • Visualization	Risk Strat • Aggregation/ETL • Enterprise DWH	HIE / QHIN • RPM • National Exchange • Home Health • Telehealth • CBO referrals • Post-Acute

Inputs / Data Sources
EHR • Claims Files – Rev Cycle • HIE / Outside Data • Dept System • SDoH • Diagnostic Devices • CRM • Clin Documentation • RPM devices

Figure 6: Vendor diversity in your organization's health IT stack

Looking at this picture, ask yourself: How diverse is our health IT stack? Is it a single-vendor-dominated organization? Do you see areas where your organization supplements the stack with modules from other firms? If you circled modules from outside firms, ask yourself why that is: Innovation? Lower cost? A better UX? Other reasons?

Matching this stack diagram to your organization's current state can show you where you have opportunities to bring in third-party modules. Your diagram can be the starting point for the discussion in chapter 7 of this book, where we'll see a phased approach to extending the stack.

Finally, write down any additional modules in the stack diagram that you would like to see added to your organization's stack. They can be in any layer of the stack, in the data source layer at the bottom, the application layers in the middle, or the user-focused layers at the top. Make a note of these future modules.

TRAJECTORY OF COST AND ROI ON HEALTH IT

Tracking the health IT cost for a hospital or physician practice is tricky and depends on many factors. For this workbook topic, we'll make some broad assumptions, focusing on trends, not exact numbers.

In the next chapter, we will discuss how large EHR vendors make it financially attractive to hospitals and practices to stick with a single vendor. Adding modules from other vendors should increase the overall cost of health IT, especially in the beginning phases. We're going to explore the trajectories of health IT spending, over time, using various unvendor scenarios.

First, let's make some assumptions. If you work for a hospital, we're going to set the EHR cost at $5,000 per bed for the current year, with a slight increase each year. If you're at a physician practice, we'll set the cost at $20,000 per provider per year. These numbers are fairly arbitrary: there are EHRs that are more expensive on a per-bed or per-provider basis, and there are less expensive EHRs. This cost also should include IT staff for maintenance, IT operations, training, and other IT-related costs.

Let's also assume that the EHR is already installed and implemented. We will skip over the initial implementation effort and look at ongoing annual costs only. We're going to pretend that the EHR has been fully in use at your organization.

Figure 7 shows various cost trajectories. The "single-vendor as-is" line shows the cost (per bed or per provider) if nothing changes and you stick with the single vendor for all health IT. The other trajectories show the cost trend for adding applications, replacing small modules, and replacing major EHR components. Chapter 7 outlines options for each of these three trajectories.

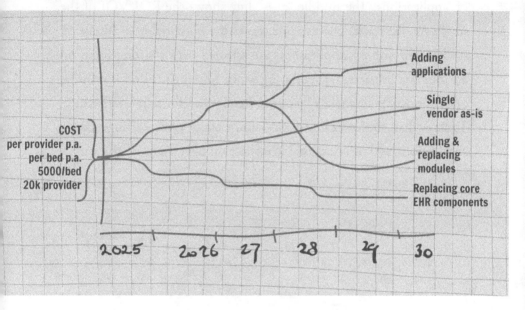

Figure 7: Unvendor project and associated cost trajectories

As you consider these trajectories, consider these questions:

- Which trajectory is your organization on today?

- If you would start to unvendor and bring in other applications, which trajectory would be both realistic and financially desirable? Is this realistic in your organization?

- If you follow the "adding applications" track, what would be your concern about impact on the organization's bottom line?

- How do you move from the "adding applications" track to the "adding and replacing modules track"?

Now let's look at Figure 8, overlaying an ROI or value on investment (VOI) trajectory, concurrent with the unvendor trajectories. We will discuss ROI and VOI in the following chapter. Both ROI and VOI measure the bottom line impact on investments, in this case in health IT applications. The middle "as-is" line shows the ROI/VOI of the single-vendor stack. The top line shows the potential of a diverse IT stack, if the add-on applications are selected with a strong focus on bottom line impacts. Unvendoring is not a hobby project. It must be underpinned by financial objectives. Remember, form follows finance. To show that, the lower line depicts nonstrategic unvendoring: adding applications with no discernable impact on operations or efficiency.

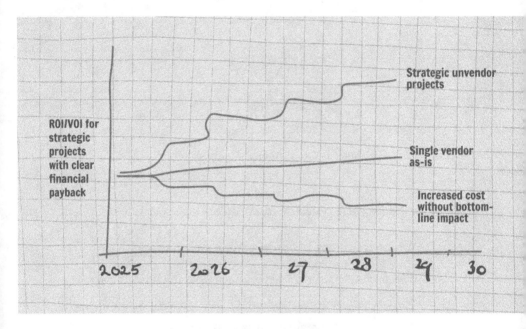

Figure 8: Unvendor project ROI/VOI trajectories

As we look at the ROI/VOI chart, let's consider these questions:

- The upper track, "strategic unvendor projects," shows a growing ROI/VOI over time. Can this be realized with either of the three unvendor strategies in Figure 7?

- What ROI/VOI trajectory would you consider both realistic and desirable for your organization?

In the following chapter, we will dive deeper into the financial ramifications of EHR contracts, and how organizations can break out of the single-vendor pricing trap. Keep the trajectories in mind, and let's pick a path that benefits our patients, our providers, and our organization's bottom line. (This, by the way, is the quickest definition of VOI!)

CHAPTER 4

BREAKING OUT OF THE
FIXED-PRICE TRAP

G ermans love to eat. They have a saying: "*Es ist bezahlt, es soll herunter*," which translates roughly as "It's been paid for, so it's going down." So it goes with the megavendor: "We're at the restaurant, the module has been paid for, so we might as well use it."

One of the hallmarks of the megavendor is the "enterprise license," the fixed-price trap that has health providers pay a fixed annual license fee. This typically includes the entire software suite and is a significant driver of the single-vendor culture. If you're having dinner with the family at an all-you-can-eat buffet restaurant, you're probably not going to the ice cream shop next door for dessert.

How do we unvendor our way out of this? Every additional module, extension, or alternative will add cost to software licensing, support fees, implementation, and support staff. It's a trap that locks health systems into single-vendor stranglehold. There are three concurrent challenges when an organization works its way out of a large single-vendor contract: high cost (both up front and ongoing), innovation stagnation, and operational inflexibility.

A single-vendor, full-enterprise contract is enormously expensive for a health system. In fact, for many health systems, a typical single-vendor contract can be the equivalent of building a new hospital wing or outpatient center. Some examples of health system outlay:

University Hospitals in Cleveland, Ohio: $400 million[30]

UMass Memorial Medical Center in Worcester, Massachusetts: $700 million[28]

NYC Health + Hospitals in New York City: $1 billion[28]

Mayo Clinic in Rochester, Minnesota: $1.5 billion[31]

Typically, the initial investment, often pulled from the capital budget, is between $2.5 million for small hospitals and $30 million for large hospitals, with an annual operating and maintenance cost of $800,000 to $3 million depending on hospital size. For ambulatory practices, either primary care or multispecialty care, the up-front investment can range from $500,000 for up to ten providers to between $2 million and $5 million for larger group practices. Annual support and maintenance fees for practices range from $250,000 to $1.2 million depending on the number of providers in the organization.[32]

As we'll see in the discussion below, with contracts of this size, it is very important to negotiate the terms in a way that doesn't lock the

---

30   Alan Condon, "University Hospitals' Epic Install to Cost $400M," December 2023, https://www.beckershospitalreview.com/ehrs/university-hospitals-epic-installation-to-cost-400m.html.

31   Jackie Drees, "12 EHR Implementations That Cost Over $100M," February 2023, https://www.beckershospitalreview.com/ehrs/12-ehr-implementations-that-cost-over-100m.html.

32   "Epic: Pricing, Reviews, and Alternatives," Tennr, accessed November 11, 2024, https://www.tennr.com/resource/epic-pricing-reviews-and-alternatives.

organization into a long-term spending plan and maintains flexibility and leverage during the contract.

With such enormous up-front and ongoing investments, once you're on this vendor's cruise ship, it's difficult to get off or change course. You paid for your ticket, and now you're in for the entire journey. And while the healthcare landscape changes, your organization is stuck, dependent on vendor support for new reimbursement or care models. All at their discretion, not yours. This causes innovation stagnation (inability to adopt new features to help support the staff's new population health model) and operational inflexibility (the vendor doesn't support new EHR diagnostic devices or new clinical documentation modules).

> **Once you're on this vendor's cruise ship, it's difficult to get off or change course. You paid for your ticket, and now you're in for the entire journey.**

I see two ways in which these high up-front and ongoing costs cause the financial trap: real and psychological. The real trap is the contract itself, and as we'll see, there are options when contracting for EHR software that give the client and buyer flexibility. The psychological trap is harder to shake off: when spending millions, sometimes billions, on software, organizations should ensure the investment pays off to maximize every benefit. Expensive purchases are like that. If I buy a Ferrari, I'll be sure to join the Ferrari fan club and grab a logoed hat and jacket while I'm at it. That's something I wouldn't do for a Toyota, even though both get me to the same destination.

Let's be real. This is about software. It is meant to help us do our work, run our organizations efficiently, and provide safe and high-quality care for patients. But it's still software—intangible, flexible, and interchangeable. Hospitals should keep an open mind, consider options for alternatives, and be willing to unvendor despite (and because of) the high costs.

What opportunities and methods do healthcare organizations have to break away from the single-vendor track, get control over cost, and regain flexibility and adaptability?

To help answer this question, I invited several of my colleagues at StarBridge Advisors (SBA) to share their experiences. SBA is a collaborative network of independent health IT advisors led by Sue Schade and David Muntz. They provide interim and fractional CIOs, CMIOs, and CTOs, and help advise and support healthcare organizations with organizational transformation and IT implementation projects. I'm joined in this conversation by Michael Glickman, SBA advisor, contract negotiator, and interoperability standards expert; David Muntz, SBA principal and health system CIO; Nayan Patel, SBA advisor and health system CIO; and Larry Schunder, SBA advisor and health system CIO, CTO, and contract negotiator.

> **Let's be real. This is about software. It is meant to help us do our work, run our organizations efficiently, and provide safe and high-quality care for patients. But it's still software—intangible, flexible, and interchangeable. Hospitals should keep an open mind, consider options for alternatives, and be willing to unvendor despite (and because of) the high costs.**

Assess Your Overall Health IT Costs

We'll start by looking at the big picture. Health IT costs are more than just fees to the software vendor. They include staffing, training, support, help desk, hardware and devices, interfaces, third-party systems, and more. A health system IT department employs hundreds of staff. The EHR vendor contract is probably the biggest ticket item in the health IT budget, especially if it's a software as a service contract, which is the most likely configuration today. But we need to also consider *all* the costs—the full picture.

Can a healthcare organization expect to reduce overall health IT cost by unvendoring and limiting their dependency on a particular vendor?

Nayan: Yes, if the organization is willing to go to a simpler system, with fewer bells and whistles, I believe they can absolutely reduce health IT spending. In my current hospital, a well-functioning rural hospital, we spend 3.5 percent of patient care revenue on IT, including staffing with a relatively small team. In comparison, my previous large health system spent 4.5 percent. That difference, for a large health system, that 1 percent reduction, could be a billion dollars.

Larry: I agree with Nayan. Yes, by switching to a low-cost vendor for all or part of their health IT solutions, they can reduce health IT spending. Gartner used to recommend a target of 3.7 percent of net patient revenue and increased that to 4.2 percent for additional security spending. I would go into my annual budget presentation and explain: this is my target according to Gartner, and here is where we're overspending and how we can reduce our overall cost.

Mike: In my opinion, if you're only looking at cost, you'll spend more on an application set from multiple vendors. But if you look at overall organizational benefit and ROI, you can increase effectiveness and efficiency. For example, if you reduce clinical burden for physicians and nurses and return two hours per day to the clinicians, the organization is saving a lot of money.

Nayan and Larry's approach takes the more direct route to cost savings: yes, healthcare organizations can reduce their overall health

IT spending by switching from expensive EHRs to more basic, low-cost EHRs, for all or part of their applications. The expectation is that lower-cost systems still fulfill the basic requirements without the bells and whistles. In addition, by strategically including third-party modules into the health IT stack, the health IT budget will increase but so does the effectiveness and cost savings in the organization overall.

Any unvendor initiative should track two metrics: the ROI (following Mike's recommendation), and the impact on overall health IT spend (per Nayan and Larry), both in software fees but also support, interfaces, and other add-on costs. A win-win unvendor project achieves a large positive ROI while simultaneously bringing total health IT spending down, over time.

Implement Incremental Changes

The process of adding other systems and components into the health IT stack starts small, with incremental steps. In chapters 6 and 7, we will go into specifics on where to start with incremental unvendoring steps. *How would you identify the starting points for introducing new systems and decommissioning obsolete or unnecessary modules?*

Nayan: We should always assess and evaluate the EHR for what the organization needs. We've added a lot of data fields, elements, and workflow processes for regulatory requirements. Maybe some of those are not needed anymore. We may need to scale down and move to a newer, smaller solution. It's a bit like a regular cleanup of your garage. For example, I bought a miter saw, and it's been sitting in the garage for ten years. I didn't even bother selling it, just donated it. The cost of keeping it is not worth it. Reevaluate your applications regularly to make sure they are critical to the organization's functioning and effectiveness, and if not, consider decommissioning them.

Larry: In addition to simplifying the applications, you can also cut down on system updates and upgrades. I would ask my vendor to give me the performance ratings, and I will maintain a technology solution that hits those ratings: storage, response time, network loads, etc. By doing this, I was able to get one to two releases behind where they were, which was worth millions of dollars in spending, because I didn't need to pay the higher maintenance and depreciation. This delay would be perpetual: Once we were able to delay $5 million over three years, we wouldn't have to spend that amount again, as long as we stayed within their performance arc.

Nayan: Large health systems face a challenge when they acquire additional facilities. They may have hospitals or clinics at different stages of implementation. But this also creates an opportunity: if they want to make a move to a different EHR or a different revenue cycle system, they can start with the new hospital; create a new, simpler model; and use that as the model for the rest of the system.

One takeaway is that incremental changes start by doing a regular needs evaluation. I think this is an important realization. During my years as a CMIO, I would always be thinking about the next module, the next new feature to activate. My team would rarely, if ever, do the opposite: What can we turn off? Applications may be obsolete or not mission critical. Before you start adding to the IT stack, take a good look to see if you can remove items first. We need to clean out the garage and do a yard sale once in a while.

How do we determine what applications or modules are unused and obsolete?

1. Ask users—they won't hesitate to tell you.

2. Obtain utilization statistics: Who is using this feature, and how often? Most EHRs can provide this data for specific modules and features. (One note about utilization statistics: for many modules, it would make sense to look at not only the data-entry usage statistics but also the data viewing statistics. For example, if users routinely enter assessments, documentation items, or template information that no user subsequently views, you can save your staff a lot of time and effort.)

3. Track regulatory requirements. If a feature was turned on to meet a regulatory need ten years ago, it may no longer be required. As the Meaningful Use and Promoting Interoperability criteria evolve, your organization may be able to reduce the regulatory burden on the clinical team.

Incremental changes, both additions and deletions, can lead you to the unvendor starting points. Remember, you can only actually reduce your health IT spend if your contract gives you the flexibility to turn modules on or off.

Before you start adding to the IT stack, take a good look to see if you can remove items first. We need to clean out the garage and do a yard sale once in a while.

Before you start adding to the IT stack, take a good look to see if you can remove items first. We need to clean out the garage and do a yard sale once in a while.

Negotiate Flexible Contracts

In getting out of the single-vendor pricing trap, negotiating flexible contracts is probably an essential recommendation.

The ONC published an excellent guidebook for EHR contracting: "EHR Contracts Untangled."[33] The guidebook prepares health provider organizations to go into the EHR negotiation well prepared, with clear demands and expectations, and from a strong negotiating position. It covers functionality, warranties, liability, service-level agreements, performance, and uptime. It also outlines expectations on interoperability and integrating with third-party products.

In the procurement recommendations, the guidebook states: "A simple but effective technique in your procurement strategy is to identify a 'Plan B'—whether it be continuing to receive services from your existing EHR vendor for an additional period or progressing negotiations with an alternative vendor.... Having the ability to walk away from negotiations immediately increases your leverage and gives your organization's decision makers options to consider when reaching a final decision." Whether you're buying a car or a home or an EHR, it's important to keep the Plan B options open, and not just as a back-pocket head fake. However, the EHR vendor will want you to declare "vendor of choice" early in the process, curtailing your Plan B options and weakening your negotiation leverage.

The ONC guidebook makes no mention of all-in-one pricing versus pricing itemized by module or application. All-in-one pricing doesn't restrict your organization's ability to add third-party modules, or to replace your large EHR vendor's module with a third-party application. In such a contract, unvendoring may not result in immediate cost reduction.

---

33   Office of the National Coordinator for Health Information Technology, "EHR Contracts Untangled," September 2016, https://www.healthit.gov/sites/default/files/EHR_Contracts_Untangled.pdf.

I asked my StarBridge partners about their experiences with EHR vendor negotiations and how to gain maximum leverage and flexibility. Here are their recommendations.

Mike: I have negotiated with the large EHR vendors many times. In your negotiations, your goal needs to be that the EHR vendor becomes your principal vendor, but not the only vendor. During the contract negotiations, you have everybody's attention, so you should negotiate all pricing, all fees up front, now that we're all focused on this.

Each contract has schedules attached—milestones, payment schedules, and testing and acceptance criteria, etc. I always include an add/delete schedule. This defines for each module the initial license price and ongoing maintenance fees. This allows you to buy each module from the vendor, at prenegotiated rates, but at the same time it allows you to carve out modules if you prefer to buy them from other vendors. You aren't paying a flat fee for the entire system, but instead have itemized pricing for the major modules. If you decide to stop using a module, and deinstall it, the add/delete schedule defines how much in annual support fees you can reduce, and in some cases if you can receive back a portion of capital costs. It really gives the customer prenegotiated flexibility on current and new modules.

The add/delete schedule also would define the percent discount from the list price we would receive for new modules—for example, a new population health module. This would be part of preferred-vendor pricing.

Larry: In my negotiations with large EHR vendors, they would bring out new modules and demand more money. I would argue against taking the module in the early release module. I'd say, "We're not taking that module; we're already outsourced with another system." I would come in with respected outside counsel and show them that the contract can't force the client to spend money on a product they don't intend to use. It would be against consumer protection laws.

It's hard to push back on some of these vendor requirements, but in my experience, with the assistance of respected outside counsel, plus the support of the organization's CEO and CFO, the vendor may not say, "You're right," but a week later you'll get a letter that you don't need to buy the module to stay in compliance with the contract. That's all you need; that's the outcome you want.

The ONC guidebook and the panelists' experiences agree: negotiate your terms up front, while you have the attention of the vendor and your organization's executive team. Keep a real and credible Plan B on the table, in the form of staying with the current vendor or considering a different vendor. An add/delete schedule, allowing you to install or de-install modules, with up-front and maintenance cost for each module, would give you maximum flexibility, and in effect neutralizes the fixed-price trap. Push back on any contract practices that violate consumer protection laws.

It's very likely that your organization is in an existing long-term contract with a vendor right now, and you're not in a position to renegotiate or change your contract terms. That's okay. You can still unvendor, mostly by using the interoperability features in your EHR. You may not get immediate payback for modules you're not using, but in the long term you'll gain vendor independence and flexibility.

Invest in Interoperability

Interoperability is a prerequisite to a diverse health IT stack. Your organization will need to spend more effort, funding, staff skills, support, and training in interoperability between systems. The "EHR Contracts Untangled" guidebook by the ONC lays out what you should expect from your EHR vendor and how to incorporate the interoperability requirements in the contract. It covers interoperability and data exchange with existing systems and with new third-party applications or modules. It specifies how to negotiate pricing for interfaces up front.

The guidebook is prescient in its promotion of interoperability. It says: "Having this flexibility is important because your EHR vendor may not offer certain types of products or services, and even if it does, you may determine another vendor has developed an innovative or better approach for your requirements. This is seen in the growing market for innovative 'plug and play' technology that can enhance the functionality and value of your EHR." The growing market for plug-and-play technology is what unvendoring is about, to move us in that direction where we're more likely to supplement our EHR with third-party components.

I asked my panel: *How should an organization invest in interoperability?*

Mike: I was one of the founders of HL7 and continue to be involved in standards organizations and developing modern interoperability standards such as FHIR. Interfaces and APIs also need to be included in the add/delete schedule we mentioned earlier, with pricing levels. If you don't include the interface costs, you will get overcharged.

David: Investing in interoperability also pertains to the organization's IT staff. It's true that a diverse health IT stack will require a stronger skill set in interface and API engineers. Current API technologies make this easier, but it still requires effort and investment for installation, testing, and maintenance. I believe it's important for healthcare providers to hire interoperability IT staff to strengthen their ability to bring in newer cutting-edge technologies.

Mike mentions his involvement in interoperability standards, and we'll do a deeper dive into the standards and methods in chapter 6. We need the EHR vendor's cooperation and support for interfaces and API connections, so the contract needs to define our interface and interoperability requirements and pricing, according to some metric or sliding scale.

The largest investment to be made is in IT staff, skilled in interoperability technologies and APIs. These are the folks who install, test, and maintain connected applications. In the best-of-breed era, programmers would configure HL7 interfaces using interface engines. Some of that still exists, and we will still use HL7 interfaces for data exchange. The real investment should be in software engineers trained in modern application interoperability using FHIR-based APIs. As David mentioned, organizations will need to hire new staff with these skill sets, in addition to training their existing staff in current API technologies.

While hiring interoperability engineers will increase health IT spending, the long-term goal is to bring down the total cost of health IT while recouping the investments through efficiencies and operational cost savings.

Focus on Long-Term Savings

We didn't get into the single-vendor situation overnight. It will take a long time to move, gradually and incrementally, toward a more flexible and innovative IT stack.

How do we measure progress on that road? What metrics and milestones should we use to track our unvendor project?

David: I've been in this industry a long time. I've been CIO at Baylor Health and Texas Health Resources, both very large health systems. I have consulted many healthcare provider organizations. Based on that, I have two essential recommendations for long-term project tracking. One, compare to *baseline*, not to *benchmark*. And second, include VOI as a tracking metric in addition to the traditional financial measures.

Let's look at each of these.

Most vendors will promise improvement based on benchmarks—industry averages on, for example, accounts receivable days, Hospital Consumer Assessment of Healthcare Providers and Systems (HCAHPS) scores, readmission rates, or ED visits per one thousand patients. But there is a difference between benchmarks and baseline. The benchmark reflects the overall industry, and that may not apply to every organization. Organizations should use their own baseline, using a metric that's important to their processes. Sometimes that is a direct measure, and sometimes an indirect measure. For example, a direct measure for the project would be to get more lab results, more referrals, and higher revenue. For an indirect measure, ask the users if they like the system they installed.

For example, I reported on the impact of an interoperability project at a large health system, a project connecting several stand-alone software systems to the main EHR. I showed that their mortality rate over the past year had dropped significantly, saving more than 1,500 patient lives. The chief safety officer was in the meeting, and he supported the findings. I call that the magic of dispassionate drama. That's the effect of using a baseline: Are we better than we were yesterday on mortality, productivity, and patient experience? Of course there were many factors at play, but IT work is part of it.

In measuring VOI, we too often use ROI, internal rate of return, or net present value, which are traditional finance-based metrics. In the example above, how would I recoup the IT investment if I left out the impact on mortality? Often, it's an intangible parameter that makes the difference. Measuring the intangibles is the real challenge in our example; the power of the mortality rate was more important than the power of the dollar value.

A detailed description of VOI is outside the scope of this book, but the US Chamber of Commerce says: "The VOI concept was first introduced by Gartner, the world's leading IT research and advisory company. VOI is defined as 'intangible assets that contribute heavily to an organization's performance.' These intangible assets include knowledge, processes, the organizational structure, and ability to collaborate. Where ROI is the measure of the tangible benefits of a project or activity, VOI is the measure of the intangible benefits of a project or an activity. (VOI includes ROI.)"[34]

For any IT project, including the long-term unvendor initiative, identify key metrics to track the project's impact. The metrics should include traditional financial measures, such as cost and full-time equivalent, and revenue but also, especially in healthcare, the intangibles. Our methodology will be to track not only the ROI but also the VOI of the project.

Benefits

Unvendoring leads to lower overall health IT costs, enhanced innovation, and increased flexibility for how our healthcare organization works. As we learned from the SBA panel, there are a multitude of factors simultaneously at play, making it difficult to attribute any improvement or incremental change to a single initiative. But we need to try.

---

34 "Move from ROI to VOI (Value on Investment)," October 25, 2012, https://institute. uschamber.com/move-from-roi-to-voi/.

Negotiating a contract should reward unvendoring, not disincentivize it. Not every organization will be able to negotiate or renegotiate their EHR vendor contract. Every ten years or so, when the contracts are up for renewal, it's paramount to realize the benefits and renegotiate the terms. Once you start the process of unvendoring by adding third-party applications and components, you'll be in a better position to change the terms. Use an add/delete schedule that gives you credit for modules you don't use. Bring your overall contract down by introducing serious competitive alternatives. Most of all, bring your contract negotiators and healthcare finance people together to create a strong multidisciplinary task force to prepare your team for the next round.

Innovation and operational flexibility make up the foundation of unvendoring. Start with small, incremental projects, and as your organization gains experience in introducing and maintaining innovative applications and modules, go for larger projects. The key here is to invest in interoperability—the tools, the methods, and the skill sets of interoperability. It's not the old HL7 anymore; the world of interoperability has changed, as we'll see in the next chapter. Interoperability is the key to innovation and flexibility, and ultimately, increased independence from your EHR vendor.

Unvendoring will not happen overnight. It is incremental and long term. Those are key concepts in this project. Define the metrics, set a baseline, and track your progress against the baseline.

My wife and I once did exactly this when kayaking in Casco Bay, Maine. She's a very strong kayaker, while I'm better at running. We crossed over to Jewell Island to camp overnight. The island was far away, and there was some tidal flow pulling us starboard. It was slow going. But Casco Bay has a lot of lobster fishing, and each lobster trap has colorful buoys identifying which lobster team the trap belongs to. Those lobster buoys became my incremental marks of progress. I couldn't tell with my eyes if we were any closer to the island, but as we passed lobster buoys, sometimes bumping against the side of the kayak, we made it to shore, one buoy at a time. Keep aiming for the next lobster buoy. You'll get to the island.

Workbook

CONTRACT REVIEW

Unvendoring is not just about introducing new technologies into your organization. It also touches on the financial consequences, and on incentives or disincentives in the contract with your main EHR vendor. Now that we have discussed multiple approaches to moving away from the single-vendor contract, let's reflect on how this might work for your organization.

Discuss these questions with your health system or practice IT team:

1. Is your organization in some form of enterprise licensing contract with your main EHR vendor?

2. What modules are included in the base contract fees?

3. Are any modules excluded or "carved out" of the base package? What are they? If they are not included in the base, what is your organization's strategy on these carve-outs?

4. Looking at the contract, do you feel the contract gives you an incentive or disincentive to unvendor?

5. Are interfaces specified in the contract? Is the contract explicit on cost and pricing of interfaces?

6. Do you see other clauses that might prevent you from adding third-party modules into your health IT stack?

MEASURING AND TRACKING UNVENDOR IMPACT

For this exercise, we're defining measures for setting a baseline and tracking the progress and impact of two unvendor projects. I will propose one of the projects, and I would like you to pick another project, real or imagined, and follow along as we track the impact on our organization's metrics.

For Project 1, I am selecting a team communication and collaboration module. Think Slack inside your EHR. I'm loosely modeling this project on the CareAlign application, which we'll discuss more in chapter 7. It is a layer on top of the EHR that helps the care team communicate and coordinate tasks in a way that teams of software engineers or project managers use Slack. Imagine that every patient is a "task" and that the team needs to work together to make sure that every patient has their next step planned out. The communication and collaboration module improves care, makes the process more efficient, avoids wait times, and improves transitions.

(All numbers below are fictitious and for project modeling only.)

I include several benefits of the module for this impact tracking exercise: reduced readmission rate, reduced adverse events resulting in reduced length of stay, and more efficient handoffs for clinical teams. For the VOI calculation, I am including the reduced readmission rate and reduced length of stay because they have an actual impact on revenue. I am not including handoff times in the VOI calculation, because even though this time savings will make clinicians more efficient, I can't claim to reduce the number of full-time equivalents.

For your selection of Project 2, try to select a relatively small, but real, project that your organization has considered, or is currently considering.

IMPACT: SCOPE, COSTS, BENEFITS	PROJECT 1: TEAM COMMUNICATION AND COLLABORATION	PROJECT 2: YOUR PROJECT
Annual software license fee	$25,000	
Annual support and maintenance	$10,000	
Interfaces—up front	$30,000	
Reduction in EHR fees	$0	
Number of users year 1	125	
Number of patients impacted per year	4,550 patients/year	
ROI (in $)	200 fewer hospital days for $600,000 cost savings	
VOI: Reduced readmit rate	Readmit rate reduction by 1.5%	
VOI: Reduce adverse events	Not tracked	
VOI: Clinician handoff time savings	1 hour per clinician per day	
VOI: Operational efficiency		
VOI: Reduced length of stay	200 days per year	

Figure 9: ROI/VOI for unvendor projects. Cost and savings numbers are fictitious and for illustration.

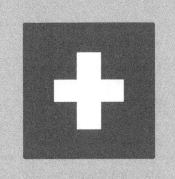

CHAPTER 5

VENDOR DIVERSITY IN THE REAL WORLD

Before we talk about how to start the unvendoring in our health systems, let's step outside the healthcare world and look at some other industries where once-dominant large vendors gradually lost their stronghold, making way for a more diverse world of products and options. Let's look at beer and coffee (both very important to many of us), food and farming, and transportation. In all these areas, consumers now have many more choices, and market forces have created a more consumer-friendly environment.

Beer and Coffee

When I moved from the Netherlands to the United States in the late '80s, the US beer scene was dominated by big brands. In a bar, there were two beer options: domestic and imported. Domestic was cheaper. Heineken was a favored brand. In my home state of Pennsylvania, the local brands were Yuengling and Rolling Rock. I'm still not sure if any of them were truly different from each other.

Today, there are three breweries in my small town of Ambler, Pennsylvania. They make great beers, with lots of styles and flavors, different hop strains, and varying alcohol levels. It's a lot of work to keep all of them in business, but somehow it's working. They are thriving, each on their own customer base. These local breweries started by selling their beers on draft in their pubs. The COVID-19 pandemic forced the brewpubs to create a drink-at-home option, and suddenly new small-batch canning technology came along. These breweries now sell their own packs of cans, with funky labels and great variety. And I'm sure you have noticed that somehow in this transition the cans became bigger—a smart way to increase the price per can without the customer complaining too much. Innovation created a strong business and a more diverse marketplace. The big brands are still in the beer store, and many consumers buy mainstream beer brands, but they are not in my fridge.

The same trend revolutionized the coffee space. Starbucks started the consumer trend away from bland mainstream market coffee. Then the local coffee shops got into the game, roasting their own local specialty coffees. Spawned by the interest in small, local coffee, there is now a thriving market in coffee-roasting machines and fancy home coffee makers. Coffee is fun, it's interesting, and it's diverse and funky. Coffee is not just about coffee; it's also about creating a space to meet and to work. I could not have predicted this development thirty-odd years ago when coffee simply meant Folgers.

Bottom line on beer and coffee: the market invented an entirely new business model, away from the big brands. It spurred innovation in brewing, branding, packaging, and consumer behavior. While consumers might not be saving money, they are getting a much better product.

Food and Farming

I love local farming. I'm a founding board member of Pennypack Farm, a community-supported agriculture farm in Horsham, Pennsylvania. Four hundred families pick up their weekly share of produce from the farm, getting hyperlocal, healthy food grown by a team of local farmers and farm apprentices. We see a similar prevailing trend toward local sustainable food and farming in many parts of the country.

Here, the change is not driven by technology. While the farm employs the latest methods in biological pest control and modern machines for small farms, the main driver here is a new business model. Customers buy directly from the farm, eliminating the retail layer. Also, customers pay an annual up-front fee for the entire season of produce, which shifts the risk of crop failure and weather events from the farmer to the consumer. As in population health, the shifting of risk from one party to another creates an entirely different business model beneficial to both sides. In analogy to VBC, you might call this the value-based farming model.

Just as we saw in the coffee and beer examples, these farms create communities, groups of loyal clients that become so committed to the concept they form a loyal support base. This client community breaks away from the big brands and the large grocery stores. Big-box stores have noticed the shift in demand toward healthy, locally grown food, and most stores today offer an excellent food variety. Best of all, despite competition from large-brand stores, the local sustainable farm model continues.

Transportation

Let's take Washington, DC, as an example of a city where transportation is unrecognizable compared to fifteen years ago. Traditional modes of transportation were dominated by large players: public transportation via bus or subway, commercial taxis, and personal vehicles. Today, those options all still exist, plus a variety of microtransport options: rideshare companies Uber and Lyft. Capital Bikeshare gives people fast and point-to-point commuting using bikes and e-bikes. Electric scooter companies Bird, Lyft, Skip, and Lime create a mess on the sidewalks but are popular ways to get from A to B. The *New York Times* calls it the "Golden Age of Weird Vehicles"[35] in New York City. Indeed, the options for getting around today are endless.

This transportation transformation owes itself to new technologies: e-bikes and e-scooters for quick and easy personal transport supported by mobile phone apps to locate, reserve, and pay for your ride.

These new transportation options have transformed the cityscape as well. Roads in DC once designed predominantly for cars now have generous bike lanes and bike-specific intersections. Innovation has a ripple effect: it changes the environment, and it changes how people use the environment.

The product world is not static. Just when we reach a situation where a market is dominated by a single vendor with a product that seems to push out all competitors, the world changes. Just as the beer, coffee, food, and transportation fields cycled from vendor domination to a diverse market with many agile disruptors, the health IT market is ripe for a similar shift.

---

35   Christopher Maag, "It's the Golden Age of Weird Vehicles in New York City," *New York Times*, June 24, 2024.

There are several important themes in these stories of unvendoring in the nonhealthcare world.

The large vendors did not disappear—Budweiser and Coors, Folgers and Starbucks, Sysco and Kroger, Ford and Toyota are still here and will continue to be here, but there are many alternatives. In the health IT stack, there is still a significant role for Epic, Oracle Health, and the other vendors, but we need to supplement and surround them with a much broader set of tools and technologies.

Technology and innovation played an important role in all industries. There are affordable and small-scale beer-canning machines, small-scale coffee roasters, and especially the micro transport explosion built around electric engines. Technologies like GPS location services and mobile phones opened the doors for innovative disruptions. The same effect will take place in healthcare once we introduce more innovations into the stack.

The transition to this diverse set of options emerged because it was driven by the consumer, demanding more variety and better quality. The same is true for health IT—unvendoring will need to start with the consumer, as we'll see in the next section.

A final note about cost: the diversification in beer, coffee, and local farms did nothing to reduce the overall cost to the consumer. The cost trend in transportation is a bit harder to track. Some of the new options are clearly saving consumers money (ridesharing versus traditional taxi), but some options offer convenience and bump price (subway versus bikeshare, for example). The reality is, in most of these examples, overall spending was up, not down, and we should have the same expectation for diversifying the health IT stack. Spending will go up initially, and maybe even in the long run, which may be fine if the ROI shows better and more efficient care and a better user and patient experience.

Workbook

One form of unvendoring can create and support other unvendor movements. If this exists in the nonhealthcare space, we may also be able to find examples in healthcare.

In your town and community, ask yourself:

- Is there a brewery and a coffee shop next to a bike trail? Do they amplify each other's business?

- Is there a bike repair shop that's also a bakery and coffee shop? Or a similar combination?

- Is there a bar inside a local hardware store? Can these two models of local business keep each other afloat? (See Harry's Hardware in Cabot, Vermont.[36])

- Does your local farmers market generate spin-off business opportunities?

- Can you think of other industries where innovation and diversification have disrupted the existing large-vendor-dominated markets?

In health IT, the scenarios track similarly:

- Your healthcare organization wants to set up a referral network to local CBOs to support your patients with social services and other nonmedical support. How would an electronic referral system not only make these referrals more efficient while strengthening the relationships and collaboration between your organizations? Could you jointly identify other services that benefit both parties?

---

36 www.harryshardwarevt.com.

- Can you see how a new mobile app for your resident teams can bring in additional communication and scheduling/teamwork options that you might not have considered?

PART THREE

LET'S DO THIS

So far, we have talked about the current state and landscape of health IT. In this section, we'll look ahead and see how the landscape is changing. There is a new interoperability ecosystem that also calls for unvendoring. There is a statement in the ONC guidebook from 2016 about growing opportunities that still has relevance today: "There is growing recognition … that EHR contracts should support and facilitate the transparent exchange of information relating to patient safety and user experiences, and that both vendors and health care provider organizations share responsibility in this area."[37]

I love the statement that "both vendors and health care providers share responsibility in this area."

There are two flavors of interoperability: internal and external. Internal interoperability is data exchange inside your own organization. This is the primary form of unvendoring that adds new systems and applications into your organization's IT stack. External interoperabil-

---

37 Office of the National Coordinator for Health Information Technology, "EHR Contracts Untangled," September 2016, https://www.healthit.gov/sites/default/files/EHR_Contracts_Untangled.pdf.

ity is connecting your organization's information systems with outside systems, for example EHRs from other health systems, national and regional data-exchange organizations, and postacute care facilities. In today's environment, external also means connecting to organizations not typically associated with healthcare but gaining relevance in the broader healthcare network. These are CBOs providing benefits counseling, food and nutrition services, housing security, and other social and community services to your patients.

When launching the unvendor journey, decide if the best place to start for your organization is internal or external, or both.

As we embark on this journey, I would like to introduce you to the "Leading Edge Acceleration Projects (LEAP) in Health Information Technology (HIT)."[38] These are great unvendor examples, and as you read the list of awardees in the past years, you will notice that the projects include both internal and external interoperability use cases. If you're unsure about where to start, this list of projects will give you some great starting points. Looking at the list of LEAP in HIT awardees, you'll notice the following:

- Every one of them uses FHIR as one of their interoperability methods. That should be no surprise to anyone in the health IT field: FHIR is the current, new tool, and the industry wants to see more implementations of FHIR.

- Many LEAP in HIT projects center on social determinants of health (SDoH) and health equity applications. These applications step outside the walls of the traditional healthcare organization and include community and social services. It's a good place to start.

---

38 "Leading Edge Acceleration Projects (LEAP) in Health Information Technology (Health IT)," accessed November 12, 2024, https://www.healthit.gov/topic/leading-edge-acceleration-projects-leap-health-information-technology-health-it.

- Some of these projects use interoperability tools to improve the quality of data, in preparation for research or AI applications. It's an interesting comment on the current state of healthcare data: we need tools to improve data quality before we can use the data for analysis or AI model training.

In reviewing this list of award-winning projects, I think they are a bit esoteric, a bit academic, and not sufficiently mainstream. I'm looking for projects that would appeal to health systems, clinics, and hospitals of every size in the country—something that you'd want to replicate immediately. I'm afraid that's still missing from this list, and that's again the reason to encourage all of us to start unvendoring.

The interoperability landscape has changed: new tools, new technologies, new methods, and new legislation for both internal and external interoperability. The only thing missing is a groundswell of projects that are both innovative and pragmatic. The future of health IT will be successful examples of entry-level, midlevel, and expert-level unvendor projects, a work in progress we'll be building together over the next five to ten years.

My hope is that some of your unvendor projects will end up on the LEAP in HIT list. Let's make that our goal, and let's do it together. While we take the first small steps in this journey, know that we are headed into unrecognizable territory, far away from the single-vendor-dominant monolithic IT environment. We will hear from others in the field how their unvendor journeys succeeded and the obstacles they encountered. We can learn from those challenges and from each other's successes and failures.

Let's go do this—together.

CHAPTER 6

THE NEW INTEROPERABILITY

B efore we consider new interoperability, we need to ask ourselves: What is old interoperability? Old interoperability methods are characterized by HL7 interfaces, which required a good amount of setup, configuration, and adjustments on the sender or receiver side. The need for work-arounds was real. Although the ideal term for interoperability is "plug and play," that was never actually the case. Interfaces require testing, support and maintenance, and changes when one of the parties has an upgrade. In short, the old interoperability works but is labor-intensive and expensive.

The goals and requirements for new interoperability are that it:

- is quick and easy to set up and maintain

- does not require extensive configuration on either the sender or receiver side

- is in line with modern web- and app-focused software environments

- is supported by all major EHR firms

- forms the technology platform for applications to connect into the health IT ecosystem, with easy access for users (clinicians and patients), and secure but easy access to data

As we move into new interoperability space, the old interoperability tools don't just go away. Both sets of tools and technologies will continue to operate side by side, giving us a richer interoperability environment and better options for the applications we're trying to connect.

	OLD (CURRENT) INTEROPERABILITY	NEW INTEROPERABILITY
Dominant technology	HL7 interfaces	FHIR APIs
Purpose	System-to-system interfaces	Connections to apps and applications
Use this when you need ...	Workhorse data transport	Focused integration
If this were public transport	City bus	Uber or Lyft
Payload	All data all patients	Select data for select patients
Push/pull	Push	Mostly pull
Data format	Transaction records and Continuity of Care Documents (CCDs)	FHIR resource objects
Configuration required	Yes—significant	No, or minimal
Testing required	Yes	Yes
Supported by EHRs	Yes—with variability	Yes, as prerequisite to certification

Figure 10: Comparison of old and new interoperability environments

In this chapter, we'll look at how the interoperability environment has changed over time, from the HL7 interfaces during the best-of-breed era, to the single-vendor period, and now the new interoperability environment in a world of connected apps and applications. It's a change in the technology environment that we live in. At the same time, it's a change in which we are the actors making the change. Without our action and participation, the change may not happen or could take longer. Regulatory and policy drivers have their impact on the transition to new interoperability, but they only go so far. It will be up to us to lead our organizations into this new space.

If this [your current data transport] was public transport, old interoperability is a city bus and new interoperability is Uber or Lyft.

Context

Besides specific technologies and interoperability standards, there are ground rules to interoperability, truisms that we need to keep in mind as we aim for effective connections between systems.

The robustness principle, called Postel's law, named after Jon Postel, an American computer scientist, says (slightly reworded): "Be conservative in what you send; be liberal in what you accept."[39] In other words, in interoperability, the sending party needs to be precise

If this [your current data transport] was public transport, old interoperability is a city bus and new interoperability is Uber or Lyft.

and follow the specifications of the communications protocol. The receiving party needs to be flexible and forgiving of slight variations

---

39   "Robustness Principle," Wikipedia, accessed November 12, 2024, https://en.wikipedia.org/wiki/Robustness_principle.

if the meaning of the transaction is still clear. In a baseball analogy, the pitcher needs to be precise and accurate, and the catcher needs to be able to catch anything coming at him.

The second phenomenon of interoperability is something I have observed in my health IT work called "too much and not enough at the same time." In many examples of interoperability, the sending system is exceedingly helpful, transferring an overload of information to the receiver. It can, however, become difficult for the receiving party to make sense of the content, and worse, the one thing the receiving party was looking for may not be there. It's too much and not enough at the same time. Examples of this are the CCD and the definition of the US Core Data for Interoperability (USCDI), which we'll discuss later.

Keep these ground rules in mind: for effective data exchange, we need to adhere to Postel's law of interoperability, while avoiding the "too much and not enough" trap.

Old Interoperability

In the beginning of interoperability technologies, during the best-of-breed era, the first generation of interoperability tools was centered around HL7 interface formats. These were event-based transactions: an event would generate a transaction, containing all relevant data fields, to one or more recipients.

For example:

- A patient registration event would send all the information about the patient to any downstream system: patient demographics, date/time of the registration, patient's physician, insurance information, next of kin, etc.

- An order for a lab, or radiology or cardiology, test would send the request to the correct department, with all relevant data fields: patient ID, test ID, date/time, ordering physician, etc.

- If a lab test was complete and the results were ready to be released, the lab system would trigger the transaction to any receiving system, with all the relevant data fields: patient ID, test ID, results, date/time stamps, normal ranges, etc.

HL7 interfaces are "push" interfaces. Triggered by an event, the system pushes an HL7 transaction to one or more receiving systems. The receiving system was programmed to receive the transaction, unpack it, and use the relevant fields to process the registration, the order or the result notification.

The HL7 standards leave a lot of room for variation. Two vendors can both be HL7 compliant, but their interfaces can be different enough that they require a significant amount of configuration work. Hospital IT staff use interface engines to configure the incoming and outbound version of HL7 so the parties can communicate: matching data fields, mapping trigger events, fixing formats, and making sure that the fields required by one system are actually provided by the other.

The rise of single-vendor systems was partially in response to the limitations and shortcomings of the HL7 interfaces. Some interfaces worked well and were able to keep sender and receiver aligned. There were cases where the interface could never quite keep up with the complexity and intricacy of the communication. The HL7 interface worked well for standard lab results but was never quite able to handle more complex result types, such as microbiology results. HL7 handled orders to radiology departments, but the complicated orders to a hospital pharmacy were too much for an HL7 interface to handle reliably. Single-vendor systems didn't have to mind the gap and were better at keeping the information in sync.

New Interoperability

In contrast to HL7 push interfaces, the new generation of interoperability tools are built around the FHIR standard. (Confusingly, the FHIR standard is also owned and administered by the HL7 organization. To avoid this confusion, I will just call it FHIR.)

What makes FHIR different, and how does it enable a new generation of interoperability? It's not my goal here to go into technical details, since there is a lot of excellent technical information in various online resources. But I will highlight the key features that make FHIR the foundation for the next generation of interoperability.

- FHIR is built for a web-based environment and easily connects to web technologies such as JSON (JavaScript Object Notation), XML (Extensible Markup Language), and OAuth (open authorization).

The word "Resources" in the FHIR name refers to the definition of commonly used items in health IT applications, such as patient, medication, allergy intolerance, or observation (this means "result" as in lab or radiology result, not observation as status of a preliminary admission), or allergy intolerance. If you're not yet familiar with FHIR Resources, I would encourage you to go to the FHIR Resources page (https://www.hl7.org/fhir/resourcelist.html), and click on a few of these resources. Review the definition of some of these, read the Scope and Usage, and study the Resource Content section. You will recognize many of the data fields you would expect to see for each of these resources. Reviewing these example resources will help you understand how FHIR allows applications to communicate and exchange data on these health-related items.

- While traditional HL7 interfaces are "push" interfaces, FHIR-based applications are mostly "pull" interfaces. An application queries an EHR or another healthcare system for specific data elements: a patient's medication or medication list, a patient's most recent lab result, current allergy, visit note, or discharge summary. The queried system doesn't respond in the typical HL7 "let me give you everything I have, and you'll figure it out" way, but returns the data as requested in the FHIR query.

- Most FHIR-based interactions are about a specific patient and send/receive data in the context of this patient. It is also possible to develop FHIR-based interfaces that exchange data for multiple patients and include larger data sets, for example, for population health or quality-measure-related queries. These cross-patient data queries are called Bulk FHIR queries. Not all EHRs today support the Bulk FHIR methodology.[40]

In comparing HL7 interfaces and FHIR APIs, an HL7 interface is like a bus or a train: it transports lots of people, and they go from one station to another, traveling to fixed end points. An FHIR API works like a taxi or an Uber or Lyft: on demand, and each application to their specific needs. Just like buses and taxis, we'll have HL7 interfaces and FHIR-based connections active simultaneously. HL7 interfaces are the workhorse push interfaces keeping systems in sync, while FHIR APIs will serve to connect mobile apps, used by patients and providers, and by linking modules on top of the EHR for specific, narrow goals to supplement and enrich the EHR functions.

---

40   SMART Health IT, "SMART/HL7 Bulk Data Access (Flat FHIR)," August 2023, https://smarthealthit.org/smart-hl7-bulk-data-access-flat-fhir/.

There are two concepts that make up the new interoperability space that are more externally focused: CCDs and the USCDI. These are essential building blocks for connecting your organization to the outside world.

CCDs[41] are payload. They are XML-structured documents, intended to facilitate the patient's transition from one provider or facility to another. They serve as the baton in the relay, and in that sense they are very effective. They also tend to become large. Sending systems err on the side of including too much information just in case the receiver requires it, which causes the "too much and not enough at the same time" scenario. The receiving system can do two things with the CCD: unpack it and store the fields in the receiving EHR or keep the CCD whole and display it to the clinician who wants to read it. Many health organizations are hesitant to include data from another site into their EHR. Viewing is more likely than unpacking and storing. If the CCDs get too large, the clinicians reviewing them may find it too cumbersome to find what they are looking for. There must be a Goldilocks perfect size for a CCD, but typically the tendency is to make them too big for their britches.

The USCDI[42] is an ONC program intended to define which data elements, at a minimum, need to be available for data exchange. EHR firms need to support the USCDI fields for FHIR queries to maintain certification. The ONC USCDI website lists the fields for each subsequent version. Starting out with a true "core" set in version 1, the set rapidly expands. Version 1 includes clinical notes in narrative text format. While IT people tend to prefer structured coded data, the clinicians often prefer narrative notes, telling them what they need

---

41   There are similar concepts such as C-CDA and CDA, but for this text I will use the term Continuity of Care Document (CCD).

42   SMART Health IT, "SMART/HL7 Bulk Data Access (Flat FHIR)," August 2023, https://smarthealthit.org/smart-hl7-bulk-data-access-flat-fhir/.

to know about a patient. In version 2 and beyond, the USCDI also includes SDoH data, including SDoH problems, goals, and interventions. This data only recently came into the spotlight for healthcare professionals, helping them identify and address health-related social needs and achieve health equity goals for patient populations.

The USCDI incrementally grows the number of data fields and EHR items that are available for interoperability. EHRs need to be able to pass these elements to other systems. FHIR apps can query the EHR for USCDI fields and expect to get the correct data in return. The USCDI defines the pick list for health systems that helps set the floor under the shareable data fields. It's perfect for a pull scenario.

Government Regulations and Private Initiatives for Interoperability

The US government, through ONC and CMS, plays a strong role in laying the groundwork for the new interoperability environment. This is not the place for a detailed review of the regulations and incentive programs promoting interoperability. The 21st Century Cures Act is the mother ship for several specific interoperability rules, including the information blocking rules, the HTI-1 rule (final)[43] and the HTI-2 rule (proposed),[44] and the USCDI requirements. These rules gradually raise the floor of what each EHR firm needs to support.

---

43   HealthIT.gov, "Health Data, Technology, and Interoperability: Certification Program Updates, Algorithm Transparency, and Information Sharing (HTI-1) Final Rule," accessed November 12, 2024, https://www.healthit.gov/topic/laws-regulation-and-policy/health-data-technology-and-interoperability-certification-program.

44   HealthIT.gov, "Health Data, Technology, and Interoperability: Patient Engagement, Information Sharing, and Public Health Interoperability (HTI-2) Proposed Rule," accessed November 12, 2024, https://www.healthit.gov/topic/laws-regulation-and-policy/health-data-technology-and-interoperability-patient-engagement.

These government regulations and incentive programs have generated several private initiatives, building upon the basic principles, and creating solutions ready for implementation. The Argonaut Project,[45] SMART on FHIR,[46] CDS Hooks, and other groups, working with the major EHR technology firms, make it easier for application developers to build apps in a way that can connect to EHRs without configuration for version mismatches. Imagine that the ONC rules regulate what LEGO blocks will look like. Argonaut and SMART on FHIR are the model boxes that help you build a train or the Starship *Enterprise*.

Brett Marquard is the managing director and project manager at the Argonaut Project. He explains how the project started with the publication of the 2013 JASON report "A Robust Health Data Infrastructure,"[47] which called for open APIs and a consistent method for using the APIs. Marquard wrote one of the core implementation guides. The Argonaut group consists of healthcare IT vendors (Allscripts, Athenahealth, eClinicalWorks, Epic, Meditech, Oracle Health), large technology firms (Apple, Microsoft, Google), health plans (Humana, Optum), and several tech-forward healthcare organizations (Intermountain Health, Mayo Clinic, Mass General, and Boston Children's).

Marquard explains, "These are the organizations that want to solve clinical workflow questions. The projects focus on infrastructure and core enabling features: How does an app download clinical data and access the clinical record?" He explains why the FHIR standard

---

45   Confluence, "Argonaut Project Home—About the Argonaut Project," June 2024, https://confluence.hl7.org/display/AP/Argonaut+Project+Home.

46   Boston Children's Hospital, "A SMART Evolution," SMART Health IT, 2022, https://smarthealthit.org/.

47   "JASON Report Task Force Final Report," October 15, 2014, http://www.healthit.gov/facas/sites/faca/files/Joint_HIT_JTF%20Final%20Report%20v2_2014-10-15.pdf.

by itself may not be enough and how the Argonaut Project aims to supplement the standard: "The FHIR standard is still pretty loose. For example, FHIR doesn't prescribe how to code and label lab results, whether we use SNOMED codes, LOINC codes, or other variations, so Argonaut provides specific guidelines, tighter and more specific than FHIR. These are the specific vital sign codes we use. We need more specificity, so that people implement it the same way, which is necessary for interoperability to succeed and be scalable."

While the tools and methods for FHIR-based interoperability are becoming well defined and widely supported by the EHR firms, there is a thriving business for interoperability firms: Redox, ELLKAY, Health Gorilla, 1upHealth, Moxe, Founda, Vorro, and more. These firms provide interoperability services for healthcare providers and payers, focusing on setup, testing, and ongoing maintenance. You might wonder, if the interoperability standards are so available, why would we need middleware to make the data exchange work? I believe this is partially a transitional business (bridging the gap while standards and tools mature), and partially a customization business, addressing client-specific requirements outside or beyond the scope of standard connections.

The stage is set. The technology and methods are ready. The government requires EHR vendors to support the FHIR APIs, and so they do. Argonaut and other groups create usable modules and implementation guides. Now it's time to bring these apps into our organizations and start the gradual process of unvendoring. The next chapter starts with small entry-level projects, with limited resource requirements and low risk of disruption, which gradually move into projects with larger impact and effect on clinicians and patients.

Please consider the following workbook topics exploring the various FHIR resources and methods, helping you visualize how these standards and methods create the connections between your mother ship EHR and the new applications you'll be including in the stack.

Workbook

WHICH LEAP IN HIT PROJECTS WOULD YOU IMPLEMENT IN YOUR ORGANIZATION?

Revisit the award-winning LEAP in HIT projects: https://www. healthit.gov/topic/leading-edge-acceleration-projects-leap-health-information-technology-health-it.

As you review the list, answer the following questions:

1. Which of these applications would you want to implement in your organization, and which would bring the biggest immediate benefits?

2. Does reviewing this list trigger ideas for other applications and unvendor projects you'd like to pursue? Jot them down here; we may need them later.

3. Does the list inspire you to pursue a similar project? Is it intimidating? Do you see your organization on this list with your interoperability project?

IMAGINE FHIR USE CASES

To demystify things a bit more, note that FHIR is just a technology standard that we can read and understand. Let's go through a few use cases and see how FHIR would support the data flow.

Revisit the list of FHIR resources: https://www.hl7.org/fhir/resourcelist.html.

USE CASE 1: AN APP TO RETRIEVE LAB RESULTS FOR A GIVEN TIME PERIOD FOR A PATIENT

- Open the Diagnostic Report content. This would give you several results, also called observations, for a patient.

- Scroll down to the Resource Content section and find the "subject" field. That's where the requesting app would pass the patient ID.

- Just underneath is the "effective" field, allowing your app to pass a point in time or a time period for the results.

- The "result" field allows your app to specify whether it wants a specific result code (for example, a glucose test), or if left open will retrieve all matching results.

- Once the server system receives this query, it will return the data in the same structure, following the Diagnostic Report resource definition, with all data that matches the query.

USE CASE 2: AN APP TO RETRIEVE A VISIT NOTE

To create this use case, we will review the Argonaut Implementation Guide for Clinical Notes (https://www.fhir.org/guides/argonaut/clinicalnotes/guidance.html).

- In this Implementation Guide, see how FHIR defines several note types, allowing the app to be specific about which notes it's retrieving.

- See how the FHIR Search function allows the app to define search parameters to allow the app user to narrow down which notes they are looking for.

Other use cases: looking at the FHIR resource page, imagine what other use cases you can build and how these resource definitions would serve as ingredients to the project.

SEARCH CAPABILITY

We mentioned the "too much and not enough at the same time" problem: a clinician needs an important piece of patient data—for example, the most recent ultrasound report performed at a different hospital, or an endocrinology visit note, or a set of lab results. Using current interfacing methods, the sending system would send a large amount of information: the complete CCD, including allergies, problems, lab results, vital signs, medications—and maybe the ultrasound report or endocrinology note. The clinician would need to scroll through a lot of information to find what she or he is looking for.

The best solution for the "too much and not enough at the same time" problem is search. If users can do a search and be specific about what they are looking for, the responding system can provide just that. For example, the doctor needs to see the patient's ultrasound report from Temple University. He doesn't need to see the patient's entire chart from Temple or from all the other health systems in the Philadelphia area, just the ultrasound report. That's not how most data-exchange systems work today. New interoperability methods will help solve the "too much and not enough" problem.

How would you design an FHIR-based app where a clinician can define what they are looking for with a simple search string of what they are looking for? How would an EHR or an HIE respond to the query? Do you see examples of "search" in your organization's EHR and HIE?

OAUTH

A diverse stack of healthcare apps is unusable if the user has to log on to each app, with various user IDs and passwords. OAuth solves this for connected apps, not just for healthcare but for any industry. OAuth is a protocol that allows one system to pass an access token to another system, giving the user the authority to use the connected app. We don't need to understand how it works, but we need to know that it exists and that it's widely used to allow users to hop from one system to another system.

HL7 FHIR uses OAuth as they launch applications. This is the key to creating a seamless experience for users while they are in fact using multiple apps or applications. It is part of the SMART on FHIR tools. Review the SMART App Launch overview here: https://hl7. org/fhir/smart-app-launch/.

Notice (in section 1.2) how the App Launch allows the connected apps to include context, such as the currently selected patient. Imagine how frustrating it would be if a clinician would have to reselect or reidentify the patient they were working on. The SMART App Launch can keep the current patient in context, creating a smooth UX as they use multiple apps.

CHAPTER 7

THE UNVENDORING JOURNEY: A PHASED APPROACH

I n my conversations with healthcare CIOs and CMIOs, I encounter many unvendor examples. Not all examples are successful, and not all of them come to fruition, but I still count them as examples of extending the function of the EHR and targeting specific business functions with add-on applications. I'm inspired by the examples, and I'm disappointed if a project failed, or worse, wasn't even started due to "road map" hesitations or other obstacles. Nevertheless, I feel it's every CMIO's and CIO's job to have at least one unvendor project on deck in their department.

In this chapter I will provide examples of unvendor projects, starting with small entry-level projects and gradually upping the game into larger projects. There is no specific order in which to take on one of these projects. There are, however, a few things to keep in mind.

For your first project, choose something that fits the following characteristics:

- Useful: Choose an application that fulfills a need currently not sufficiently met by the main vendor's system. This project will extend your current system capabilities.

- Target users: Select a project that has a distinct and identifiable group of target users who would be eager to work with you. Think of medical residents, care coordinators, physicians in a specific department or specialty, or a specific subgroup of patients.

- Narrow technical needs: The ideal project requires a limited set of data to be exchanged, and a narrow set of interaction points between the new application and EHR platform.

- Business case: A good starter project has a well-defined and easy-to-measure impact on staff productivity, clinician experience, and the organization's bottom line.

Before you start, put together a team to take on this project. It doesn't need to be a large team, but it's essential to have key players on board. Think of this team not only as the group to implement the first unvendor project, but the team that will become skilled at interoperability and connected applications. While implementing your initial projects, you're investing in this team's skill set and building your organization's capacity for diversifying the IT stack. This team should include the following:

- Project sponsors who will champion the project up and down the chain of command. Depending on the app or application, this might be any combination of CMIO, CNIO, CIO, CMO, and/or CNO, or anyone else with leadership visibility in the organization.

- Project owner(s) who will coordinate day-to-day progress on the project and remove obstacles if necessary.

- User champions: A small representation of the user group your project aims to serve. They need to be champions in two ways: support the project's goals and objectives, and be seen as champions by their peers, leaders with recognized respect and ability to represent the group.

- Tech team: The application support team, interoperability engineers, data analysts, data and network security engineers, and the informatics team help in the design, rollout, and training if necessary.

During the initial and subsequent projects, remind your team and your organization's executives why you're doing this. This is not just about the merits of your first application. The first and second projects are investments in long-term flexibility, innovation, and competitive advantage to the organization. You're doing this to futureproof your organization by building a more resilient and sustainable IT stack. Keep communicating the larger goals while working on smaller near-term objectives.

Interoperability in general is difficult, requiring a decision-making matrix that involves all three legs of the stool: operations, clinical, and technology.

Phase 1: Start and Extend

Phase 1 projects emphasize adding new capabilities to the existing EHR. This is the "supplement" phase. In these examples, we're adding user interface applications, connected devices, telehealth capabilities, and data exchange to external organizations. It's all about adding new growth to the tree. Pruning comes later.

CLINICAL DOCUMENTATION:
DAX, ABRIDGE, SUNOH

Ever since Sinsky's finding that clinicians spend approximately 50 percent of their time doing clinical documentation both during patient visits and after hours,[48] there is a push for reinventing clinical documentation.

Old-school thinking: Every field must be structured for data analytics; documentation templates are comprehensive for clinicians to capture important data. Result: unreadable notes, time wasted on data capture, and clinician burnout.

New-school approach: Use modern technologies and AI tools to assist in clinical documentation, shift from structured data capture to narrative text, and make notes available to patients. Result: less time spent on clinical documentation, improved communication with other clinicians and patients, and no noticeable loss in data for analytics and billing.

The key to this shift is the use of modern clinical documenta-tion tools, assisted by AI algorithms. Nuance's DAX system, Abridge, or eClinicalWorks's Sunoh system are examples of ambient scribes or ambient clinical documentation systems. These systems capture doctor-patient conversation with one or multiple microphones in the patient room, and use generative AI methods to compose a visit note in the traditional subjective, objective, assessment, and plan structure, or similar. For example, a team at the Permanente Medical Group in

---

48 C. Sinsky et al., "Allocation of Physician Time in Ambulatory Practice: A Time and Motion Study in 4 Specialties," *Annals of Internal Medicine* 165, no. 11 (September 2016).

California found that physicians using an ambient AI scribe tool spent significantly less time doing documentation during the visit and after hours.[49] They quote some of the physician users: "I use it for every visit … it is making my notes more concise and my visits better…. This has been the biggest game changer for me," and "I even had a patient praise the fact that I could listen instead of type during the visit." The study found that the quality of the ambient AI–generated notes was substantially equivalent to physician-generated notes.

The Permanente team also identified challenges and hurdles of introducing ambient AI documentation. They recommend, "It is essential to have clinical champions to overcome barriers to adoption and to foster an organizational culture that supports innovation." This is precisely why it is so important to bring innovative documentation tools into the organization. The technology evolves fast, and it's easy to assume that it's better to wait until the technology matures. I disagree. Get in on the ground floor, reap the direct benefits for users and patients, and bring the culture of innovation and cutting-edge competition into the organization.

Many larger EHR firms have set up integration points to this technology.

---

49   A. A. Tierney et al., "Ambient Artificial Intelligence Scribes to Alleviate the Burden of Clinical Documentation," *NEJM Catalyst Innovations in Care Delivery* 5, no. 3 (2024), https://doi.org/10.1056/CAT.23.0404.

Use Case: Clinical documentation, ambient AI scribe

Interoperability: FHIR APIs

Benefits: Reduced documentation burden, improved clinician experience, improved patient experience, increased clinical efficiency

Challenges: Clinician learning curve, need to review and verify AI scribe–generated notes, privacy concerns, organizational hesitance to move into rapidly developing technology

TEAMWORK, TASK MANAGEMENT, COLLABORATION: CAREALIGN

Subha Airan-Javia is a physician at Penn Medicine and the cofounder and CEO of CareAlign. Subha created CareAlign as a project management and teamwork system for healthcare teams. She compares it to "Jira and Slack for clinicians." Software engineers use Jira and Slack (or similar collaboration platforms) to collaborate with their coworkers, ask questions, post updates, and keep moving toward their deadlines and deliverables.

CareAlign does the same thing for healthcare teams of hospitalists and residents. EHRs typically have a patient-centric view: they capture and store the patient's clinical data, orders, medications, notes and documents—one patient at a time. CareAlign allows clinical teams to look at their panel of patients and monitor the many tasks and updates throughout the day and night: new results, new orders, medication changes, pending tests, and target discharge dates. This process relies on data from the EHR but adds a layer of coordination and project management.

I asked Dr. Airan-Javia what interoperability methods CareAlign uses to connect to the EHRs. She said, "We want to be as flexible as possible. The UI layer can ingest APIs from multiple different sources. They can be FHIR, or vendor-specific, we can also take HL7 transactions, or CCDs. Most organizations have not yet turned on the FHIR APIs, so many will just take the HL7 interface options." Clearly, this is a work in progress. For interoperability to become scalable and available to most health systems, there is still work to do to activate and enable API capabilities in the EHRs.

According to Dr. Airan-Javia, organizations using CareAlign have increased HCAHPS patient satisfaction scores, realized a 75 percent reduction in preventable errors, and saved clinicians approximately one hour per day through more efficient task management and communication.[50]

There are other similar project management tools: Dock Health (more ambulatory focused), or generic project management and teamwork applications such as Trello by Atlassian, Asana, and others.[51] Some may have EHR integration points, but, even without EHR integration, project management can still make the handoffs smoother and the team more effective. Airan-Javia says: "Where residents and hospitalists today use Excel and Google docs, you're probably better off using a real project management system."

---

50   CareAlign Overview at carealign.ai; personal communication with Dr. Airan-Javia.

51   "Best Project Management Software of 2024," Forbes Advisor, updated November 28, 2024, https://www.forbes.com/advisor/l/top-project-management-software.

> **Use Case**: Teamwork, task management, collaboration, and communication for inpatient or ambulatory clinical teams
>
> **Interoperability**: FHIR APIs, HL7, CCDs
>
> **Benefits**: Reduced readmissions, reduced length of stay, higher patient satisfaction, better clinician experience
>
> **Challenges**: Organizational hesitance to have a third-party UI layer on top of the EHR; resistance to unvendor—not having the interoperability layer activated and enabled

CONNECTING DEVICES: ARGONAUT AND BEYOND

AI technology is empowering a new range of smart healthcare devices. Patients use smart devices for continuous glucose monitoring (CGM). Clinicians use point-of-care devices, such as smart stethoscopes and portable ultrasound devices, for rapid examination and diagnosis. These devices present revolutionary changes to patient care, and we need to have a plan to incorporate these devices into the IT stack.

How do smart devices differ from conventional patient data devices?

- They have electronic data output, either as a continuous data flow, or as a set of clinical data points, or both.

- The AI algorithm adds a level of clinical interpretation on the data—distinguishing arrhythmias, heart and lung sounds, and other clinical findings.

- They allow point-of-care physicians in primary care offices and EDs to perform diagnostic tests that would previously require a radiology or cardiology testing referral.

And importantly for our project, most of these devices include the ability to exchange data using FHIR APIs or device-specific APIs.

One of the Argonaut 2024 priority projects is creating APIs to write results or vital signs from a device into an EHR. The specific focus is on CGM devices, but the method is generic and would work with other devices that capture patient vital signs. Brett Marquard, the managing director and project manager at the Argonaut Project, is excited about connecting CGM data into the EHRs.

The main device manufacturers Dexcom, Medtronic, and Abbott are on board, and the main EHR vendors are at the table. He says: "I'm very proud of this Argonaut Project. We bring together vendors with a shared problem that we're trying to solve and improve. It's a unique, collaborative industry activity from the health tech vendors. People sometimes underestimate the power that health systems have to influence these vendors, and this project shows they should start using that power."

A key element of the CGM data upload is that it doesn't upload raw data, which would overwhelm clinicians and detract value and insight to the data. Instead, the devices upload an Ambulatory Glucose Profile report, a seven- or fourteen-day summary of CGM results with trends, target zones, time in range, and peaks and valleys. This adds value to the data for patient and provider.

Device data upload may start with the Argonaut's CGM project but has many other applications as devices "get smarter" and include AI algorithms. One would not typically consider uploading traditional stethoscope sounds, but the Eko line of smart stethoscopes adds data interpretation and includes FHIR APIs to upload the data to the EHR and patient record.

Butterfly point-of-care ultrasound devices are used by PCPs and ED physicians, leading to a faster point of care without sending the patient to the imaging department. Butterfly devices and similar portable ultrasound devices include FHIR APIs to upload results to the patient's record, where they can be viewed and shared by other providers. Brett Marquard says: "We start with a narrow path, say for a skier, for CGM data, and then we plan to make that path wider, the width of a car, so that you can send the point-of-care device through it."

These devices come at the right time for VBC practices: fast and accurate data, which can at times avoid expensive and time-consuming referrals, imaging studies, or observation admissions.

Old-school thinking: Results come from the lab and the imaging department, using an HL7 interface.

New-school approach: Data comes from many smart devices, either worn by the patient or used at the point of care. I see tremendous growth in these smart devices and hence the need to connect them into the data infrastructure, starting with CGM data and scaling up from there.

However, one important aspect of device data exchange should be solved. We need an efficient way to identify patients whose data is being transferred. According to Marquard, this is a challenging problem that may require a variety of workflows. Some organizations use a "device bar" where users can connect to their patient record. QR codes can help link the device to the patient. Marquard thinks room sensors or proximity sensors can provide the patient ID, and he stresses the importance of an efficient workflow to connect device data to the right patient.

Use Case: Device data exchange—starting with CGMs and scaling up to other smart devices

Interoperability: FHIR APIs

Benefits: Data exchange from many patient and provider devices into the EHR

Challenges: Patient identification; need for increased standardization and easier setup and maintenance

TELEHEALTH AND SCALABILITY: PROVIDENCE HEALTH

Most of us are familiar with the ambulatory version of telehealth: the patient at home, connecting to their doctor or caregiver via a telehealth connection. Providence Health, based in Seattle, Washington, has built an extensive network of telehealth physicians focused on inpatient specialist consults. Dr. Eve Cunnigham, chief of virtual care and digital health at Providence, leads the project. Providence has just shy of one hundred hospitals, in five states, ranging from large tertiary-care centers to smaller rural hospitals. They provide telehealth inpatient consults for neurology, infectious diseases, intensive care, and cardiology.

Dr. Cunningham describes the process: "When a patient requires a consult, we bring in a telehealth workstation on wheels and beam the specialist into the room. We have three neurologists covering ninety-two hospitals on Telestroke. We don't need ninety-two neurologists on call, only three. They do 20,000 tele neuro consults per year for inpatients.

"For stroke patients, approximately 70 percent of the time we can keep the patient in their community hospital and don't need to transfer the patient to a tertiary center. That benefits the patient, it benefits the community hospital by keeping the patient, and it doesn't clog up the already busy tertiary care center. It's a great example of better care, better financial outcomes, and better patient experience."

Providence Health initially built their own solution for telehealth consults: placing the order, assigning the consult to the appropriate physician, and using scheduling and credentialing logic. It turned out to be too cumbersome, requiring too many steps. They now partner with software firm Andor Health and streamlined the process into fewer steps and an easier workflow. Dr. Cunningham explains: "We built a no-code environment where the regions can build and maintain their own department sand clinician directories. This allows us to move more quickly. It is critical to empower the workforce to build out digital infrastructure to enable clinical care. We can't rely on a single EHR analyst to build this. Just like in other industries, we created enablement platforms to build out the digital experiences at a more local customized level rather than centralizing everything with limited resources."

For a large healthcare organization such as Providence, this telehealth solution allowed them to dramatically scale the availability of specialty consults across their hospitals. What works for ninety-two hospitals can also work for five or ten hospitals, with the same benefits: fewer specialists supporting consult across multiple sites, with shorter wait times, allowing each department to work at the top of their clinical capabilities. EHR vendors may not support the workflow, but Providence has shown how to create an EHR-linked workflow solution that makes tele consults available across the health system.

Use Case: Telehealth for inpatient consults

Interoperability: FHIR APIs, HL7 transactions, and custom data uploads for scheduling, credentialing, etc.

Benefits: Dr. Cunningham: "We have a set of ROI calculations and KPIs around each service line. Hospital throughput and capacity is up. We maintain higher acuity for tertiary care hospitals. The tele psychiatry can discharge 30 to 40 percent of cases directly from ED, requiring fewer hard to find beds."

Challenges: Again Dr. Cunningham: "Leadership mindset. Clinicians understand things differently than nonclinicians. IT people don't always understand clinical operations and may not see what problem we need to solve. Also, the person who owns the relationship with the EHR vendor should not be incentivized by the vendor's loyalty programs. Interoperability in general is difficult, requiring a decision-making matrix that involves all three legs of the stool: operations, clinical, and technology. We need to take a strategic view that includes the benefits for care delivery, ROI, patient, and clinician experience."

FROM HEALTH INFORMATION EXCHANGE TO COMMUNITY INFORMATION EXCHANGE

So far, the unvendor examples above were additions to the internal stack, the tools and applications inside your organization. This final project in Phase 1 looks at external diversification. Most healthcare organizations can exchange clinical data with other healthcare organizations through one or more of these networks:

- EHR vendor-supported networks, such as Epic's Care Everywhere or Oracle/Cerner's Commonwell Health Alliance. These networks often also include data and transactions from other EHRs. These vendor-sponsored networks will now transition to Qualified Health Information Networks under the Trusted Exchange Framework and Common Agreement architecture.

- Regional HIEs. Every state in the US has one or more HIEs, and many hospitals and practices are connected to their HIE to exchange clinical data. The most common method of data sharing is in the form of CCDs, sent to the HIE at the end of a visit or inpatient stay.

- National networks, such as eHealth Exchange, which connect regional HIEs and allow hospitals to fetch clinical information from other hospitals where a patient may have had an encounter.

For this case study of diversifying the IT stack external to the organization, assume your organization is already connected to one or more of these three networks, and ideally an active data-exchange member with your regional HIE. Regional HIEs play an important role in giving providers a full picture of a patient's data and which providers are in the patient's team of caregivers.

Consider HealthShare Exchange, the Philadelphia regional HIE. HealthShare Exchange estimates that 50 to 60 percent of patients with chronic conditions, such as diabetes or osteoporosis, also see other providers outside the organization's network, with different EHRs. It's important to be able to access data from these "outside" providers, and it's the role of HIEs to make that data exchange possible.

Because of changes in reimbursement and care models (see chapter 2), the data-exchange network expands even further to CBOs. Socioeconomic determinants play a major role in a person's health and well-being. Behavioral, social, and environmental factors can determine 60 percent of a patient's health status.[52] Providers now routinely collect information about a patient's socioeconomic status, called SDoH. EHRs now have templates to collect SDoH data, and the USCDI includes SDoH data to enable data exchange.

Pennsylvania's PA Navigate project is an example of using SDoH data to refer patients to one or more CBOs, expanding the care network outside the traditional physical health providers to include community organizations, which are much better equipped to assist patients with the social and economic issues.

HealthShare Exchange's CEO Marty Lupinetti describes the project: "PA-Navigate is opening the view so you can see which CBOs patients are being referred to. We see the whole picture. If someone is already dealing with food insecurity, that means I can focus on the housing. It reduces duplication of effort. The project puts the HIE in the center of the network, so we can bring that information back to the caregiver. Now providers will know if the patient actually went to that organization, if they completed the program, whether

---

52   J. M. McGinnis, P. Williams-Russo, and J. R. Knickman, "The Case for More Active Policy Attention to Health Promotion," *Health Affairs (Millwood)* 21, no. 2 (March–April 2002): 78–93, https://doi.org/10.1377/hlthaff.21.2.78, PMID: 11900188.

the assistance was successful. We call this a closed-loop referral: the information circles back to the patient's care team."

Lupinetti continues to describe challenges with including CBOs into the data-exchange network: "We're dealing with the full spectrum of capabilities, from mature CBOs with IT infrastructure that can process intake, a referral, and respond with information to the provider. At the other end of the spectrum there may be a small organization in a church basement or a community center, with limited resources, where the team will need some workflow or step to log into the portal, register a person, and track information. The most interesting thing about this project is that it expands the traditional HIE into what I call a community information exchange (CIE), creating a much broader network of players, all coordinating their services to improve the healthcare and well-being of the patient."

Use Case: Extending data capture outside the healthcare organization to other regional healthcare providers and to CBOs for services to patients with health-related social needs

Interoperability: HL7, CCDs, custom APIs and interfaces

Benefits: Fast and efficient access to patient data from other providers; including CBOs in the patient's care network and closing the CBO referral loop by bringing social services information back to the care team; benefits include sharp reductions in the use of acute care

Challenges: Wide variety of technology platforms in CBOs; data standardization and adherence to standards both in healthcare organizations and CBOs

Phase 2: Technology Diversity

The Phase 1 examples are starting points on a path to a more diverse health IT stack. These projects bring in new applications and new interoperability needs into your organization and set the stage for bigger projects. IT staff have learned from building and maintaining Phase 1 projects, and they are prepared to take on larger-scale applications. If you tracked the impact on your Phase 1 projects on ROI, on patient or provider experience, and clinical metrics, and the impacts gave you a success story to tell, you're creating an appetite for more.

Phase 2 proposes unvendor projects that not only add new technologies to the stack, but also can replace or substitute some existing EHR functions. Most of these projects can live side by side with existing EHR function, but we're going to move from "in addition" to "instead of." It's the next step toward independence from the single vendor.

POPULATION HEALTH MANAGEMENT AND BECOMING A PAYVIDER

If your practice includes a significant number of patients under a VBC contract (chapter 2 Workbook, Health Care Payment Learning and Action Network categories 3 and 4), then this is the project for you. You are likely already using tools to manage your at-risk population, your "panel." That can be an Excel file, a Google Docs shared document, or the population health tool inside your EHR. Or you can unvendor and use a third-party application connected to your EHR and other data sources.

EHRs are built around the patient, with the clinician as target user. Population health management applications are built around a panel, with the care team as target user. EHRs are one on one, while population health requires many for many.

Population health management is a busy space with a large choice of applications. Some are built into EHRs, and many are EHR independent. Some are more focused on health plans; others are more focused on ACOs and practices. Some are heavy on data analytics; others are more focused on care coordination and team workflow. Some do it all. With so many players in this field, unvendoring starts with a vendor comparison using a market research firm.

Medecision is a population health system with a slight slant toward health plans. CMO Katherine Schneider emphasizes the importance of data and analytics: "We need to be able to take in data from multiple sources, EHR data, claims data, enrollment data, data from HIE, and more. The ability to take in data, scrub it, and get it ready for analytics and driving the care process is the top priority for our clients. This is what drives the care coordination and utilization management workflows."

Aneesh Chopra founded Care Journey, a patient engagement app that is now part of the Arcadia population health management system. He explains the need for a population health system side by side or on top of the EHR: "If I take risk, if I'm an ACO, I'm not asking the question about the patient in front of the doctor. I'm worried about the 99 percent of the patient panel *not* in front of the doctor. And that requires a design principle, which is permissive in sharing, not restrictive. I want to grab any signal, any data point, to determine which patients I need to focus on, out of my entire panel. To get that accurate list, I need to be more permissive on ingesting and aggregating outside data. The demand signal from doctors who are in risk contracts requires engineering with a focus on interoperability, to build bridges toward a connected world."

Oak Street Health has built their own homegrown Canopy population health system, working side by side with its commercial EHR. Most Oak Street clinicians are comfortable working in both spaces at once, but it is critical for the optimal workflow to provide tight integration and single sign-on access.

Population health and VBC is where business models, care models, and technology models come together. It is also the area in which innovation and flexibility move fast. This is the primary area where you don't wait for your EHR megavendor to build it. Sign a short-term contract with a third-party firm. When your EHR vendor catches up, you can consider switching to their platform. There is no shame or failure in switching applications, and your team will have gained valuable experience.

Use Case: Care coordination for a panel of patients, with a team of care providers, in a VBC setting

Interoperability: Extract, transform, load (ETL) for analytics data, FHIR for connected apps, custom integrations

Benefits: Patient panel risk stratification, prioritized care management, team-focused care coordination, analytics, and metrics

> **Challenges**: Workflow integration between popula-
> tion management and patient record; most users
> use both, so this connection is critical.

CLINICAL DECISION SUPPORT

At the outset of my career in informatics and health IT, clinical DS was the most important thing. Helping physicians and clinicians make better decisions. That was the ultimate goal of our entire field and our science. I wasn't the only one thinking this: there are CDS committees, work groups, CDS standards, and CDS collaboratives.

And what is the first reaction from many clinicians? Alert fatigue. Too many messages and interruptions, many of them well intended but irrelevant or unimportant. Approximately 90 to 95 percent of CDS messages are overridden by the user.[53] Many factors create this high rate of overrides, and we need to do better. I wrote about the "too much and not enough at the same time" phenomenon in chapter 6, and it plays a role in CDS: too many alerts and reminders obscuring those that actually matter.

I have not given up on the promise and potential of CDS. Despite, or actually because of, these worrisome utilization statistics, we need to keep working on this. Unvendoring can help improve the state of CDS, but we need to rethink our approach.

Old-school thinking: Every healthcare organization writes and configures their own CDS rules in their EHR's rules engine. This is labor-intensive for the informatics team and for clinicians who validate clinical rules. Locally configured CDS is less accurate,

---

53   T. N. Poly et al., "Appropriateness of Overridden Alerts in Computerized Physician Order Entry: Systematic Review," *JMIR Medical Informatics* 8, no. 7 (July 20, 2020): e15653, https://doi.org/10.2196/15653, PMID: 32706721; PMCID: PMC7400042.

specific, up to date, and user-tailored than professional, shared CDS knowledge sources.

New-school approach: A hospital's informatics team shifts their focus to curating CDS knowledge from outside sources. Hospitals do not need to reinvent the wheel each time. CDS Hooks and Smart on FHIR apps are two ways to benefit from the work and experience from other organizations and scale up CDS.

Dr. Kensaku (Ken) Kawamoto is the associate CMIO and vice chair for clinical informatics at the University of Utah in Salt Lake City, Utah. He is an expert on CDS standards, including CDS Hooks and Smart on FHIR apps. He explains the difference: "CDS Hooks is a set of FHIR APIs in the EHR that call decision rules from outside knowledge sources. Smart on FHIR has a set of CDS applications that use FHIR to connect into the EHR, for example a lung-cancer screening shared decision-making app, or an app with the most common medical calculations. CDS Hooks creates a better 'inside the EHR' experience. Smart on FHIR CDS is very modular and easy to implement. Both methods shift the job of the IT team from writing logic to curating CDS applications."

A study by Kawamoto's team concludes: "Valuable digital health innovations can be implemented across health systems using only the US Core FHIR APIs that are widely supported across EHR systems."[54]

If the future of CDS is curating rather than creating clinical logic, we need external sources of CDS logic through commercial or not-for-profit shared initiatives. One example of these is Stanson Health, founded by Dr. Scott Weingarten, and now part of Premier's PINC AI DS products. Stanson's content focuses on quality improve-

---

54   K. Kawamoto et al., "Establishing a Multidisciplinary Initiative for Interoperable EHR Innovations at an Academic Medical Center," *JAMIA Open* 4, no. 3 (July 31, 2021): ooab041, https://doi.org/10.1093/jamiaopen/ooab041.

ment, reducing waste, and avoiding unnecessary care—in line with the "form follows finance" motto that drives VBC organizations.

Shifting CDS from homegrown logic in the EHR rules engine toward external and shared data sources is a gradual process. Both can and should coexist at the same time, and as the team's experience grows, the emphasis will shift from homegrown to external. This is also an area for regional or national collaboration. Kawamoto says: "We should band together different groups and share how we do CDS. I'm not sure why we don't already do this. For example, during a recent blood culture tube shortage, hospitals were writing reminders on their own rather than sharing the approach."

Start locally, act globally. By banding together and deploying shared effective CDS, we can move CDS from alert fatigue to the promise of improving clinician decision-making.

Use Case: Shifting clinical DS from homegrown logic to external CDS applications and knowledge bases

Interoperability: CDS Hooks, Smart on FHIR

Benefits: Improving the quality and scaling the use of CDS in healthcare; improving UX, reducing alert fatigue; less is more: fewer alerts and reminders, with greater impact on clinical care, utilization, and population health

Challenges: Technological challenges, hospital spending priorities, mindset around external logic vs. internally developed rules; this is a "start small and go incremental" initiative.

PATIENT ACCESS, DIGITAL FRONT DOOR: PHREESIA

Step 1 in every EHR is patient registration and appointment scheduling, also known as patient intake management or patient access. It's the patient's front door into your practice and into the EHR. In most EHRs, patient access is not sexy. It's simply gathering the patient's name, address, and demographics and setting them up for a visit. Why would this be a topic to unvendor?

Evan Roberts, Phreesia's COO, explains: "Health systems choose Phreesia because it delivers a consistent, digital-first patient journey across every care setting and service line. Phreesia gives them scalable, automated tools for patient intake and engagement, including registration, access, outreach, revenue cycle management (RCM), clinical services and operations, and more—all without adding more staff."

In other words, if your organization uses different registration systems for different departments or services, Phreesia can bring those together into a single point of contact for patients. It also emphasizes self-service, reducing the burden on your staff. It's a more efficient digital front door and lobby.

Patient intake is obviously the point of entry. Phreesia then uses the connection with the patient to continue the relationship and continue the conversation. Data Science Director Luke Goetzke's engineering team uses the data to help care teams engage patients, prompt them with timely and relevant messages, and address gaps in care—fast, efficient, and in line with the expectations of how people use digital tools to manage every aspect of their lives.

Use Case: Patient intake management, patient access—registration, scheduling, billing, payments

Interoperability: HL7 and custom interfaces

Benefits: Patient experience, self-service, automating administrative functions

Challenges: Evan Roberts: "Health systems are complex organizations, and spending the money and resources to add new technology can be a hard decision, especially when a system is leaning heavily on their EHR to meet their needs." That's the unvendor challenge in a nutshell.

ROBOTIC PROCESS AUTOMATION: UIPATH

When Siemens acquired SMS in 2000, they started developing a new EHR on a new technology platform. One key component was a workflow engine, or business process management system, to configure and automate many of the clinical and administrative healthcare processes. The workflow engine was TIBCO's industry-leading system. It posed one of the most innovative and interesting questions for healthcare organizations: How can we automate and accelerate internal processes in our organizations, such as ordering tests and medications, admitting and discharging patients, documenting and coding records, patient-tailored meal services, bed turnaround and room cleaning, and more? Many of these processes today rely on person-to-person communication.

I was a product manager in charge of embedding the workflow engine into clinical workflows. My colleague and friend Larry

McKnight reminded me: "Harm, you imagine that a hospital works like a car factory where you can automate repetitive tasks, but it's not that at all. It's more like a car repair shop where you really can't automate processes and need to rely on staff." He had a good point, but I believe that even though every patient has different needs and courses of action, there are many processes in any health setting, both inpatient and ambulatory, where business process management and RPA can speed things up and avoid things falling through the cracks.

The "R" in RPA stands for robotic—it uses software robots, or "bots," to automate tasks typically performed by humans. The bots mimic human-computer interactions to perform tasks at high volume and speed, with minimal error. I asked Jackson Rhoades, who works in the Payer, Provider, and Life Sciences vertical at UiPath, how their RPA bots interact and integrate with EHRs. There is an interesting point here: besides traditional interfaces and FHIR-based APIs, the bots are a form of interface, emulating a human user entering or retrieving data, completing steps in a process. Think of bots as another form of system interoperability.

RPA and AI are a powerful combination. On the output side, large language model AI creates great patient-facing or provider-facing applications—think of messaging, reminders, inbox management. Process mining works on the discovery, design, and optimization side, detecting and analyzing existing processes and understanding how to redesign and automate an efficient RPA implementation.

RPA is more a tool than a specific solution. Today, most RPA-based applications are in revenue cycle and administrative areas: appointment scheduling, chart completion, claims denials, prior authorizations. RPA also speeds up IT management: testing, account updates, and software updates. It will be interesting to see if

RPA can help organizations manage a more diverse IT stack, which would help address the concern about maintenance of a multivendor IT ecosystem.

Most interesting, though, will be the use of RPA in clinical care and operations. There are many promising application areas: clinical documentation, inbox management and message handling, test order fulfillment and medication orders and administration, care coordination, and discharge management and transitions. All these are currently initiated in the EHR, but insufficiently managed, orchestrated, or coordinated. There still is a lot of human work, and human inefficiency, in clinical operations. The fact that all these workflows start and end in the EHR makes clinical operations a promising point of adding RPA optimization.

In my list of unvendor opportunities, RPA is at the top spot. It's an area ripe for innovation, competitive improvement, and most importantly reducing the EHR burden on clinicians by taking over mundane and repetitive tasks.

Use Case: Process automation of frequent repetitive tasks—clinical, administrative, operational, and revenue cycle

Interoperability: FHIR APIs, traditional interfaces with payer systems using the X12 standard, and UI automation, by mimicking a human user

Benefits: faster, more efficient processes, fewer delays, reduced human work on mundane work steps

Challenges: RPA is a skill, an expertise. Just purchasing and installing the tool is not enough. The organization needs to bring in skilled process automation engineers, who work in conjunction with the clinical and revenue cycle IT teams, to redesign and optimize processes. Not every process is a candidate for RPA. This requires an innovative approach to how your organization works.

LOOK FOR BOTTLENECKS AND PROBLEMS TO SOLVE

There are hundreds of technologies and applications that would fit in the technology diversity phase of unvendoring. I only listed a few representative and promising examples, but this is by no means an exhaustive list. The HIMSS or HLTH symposiums have vendor exhibits with many innovative and creative solutions. The KLAS research website (klasresearch.com) is a great resource to see what vendors operate in a specific application space. And learn from each other's projects—in Epic founder and CEO Judy Faulkner's words, "Imitate to innovate."[55]

Identify a bottleneck in your organization and use that as a starting point for an unvendor solution. A bottleneck can be an overworked team, a group of clinicians experiencing burnout, a waiting room with unacceptable waiting times, or care gaps that persist despite the best efforts from the care coordination teams. When you find a problem,

---

55   Fred Bazzoli, "Where Will Healthcare Be in 2 Years...20 Years? Epic's Judy Faulkner Shares Insights," Health Data Management, March 14 2022, https://www.healthdatamanagement.com/articles/ where-will-healthcare-be-in-2-years-20-years-epics-judy-faulkner-shares-insights..

don't fix a small problem. Find a big problem, something that's worth fixing and is a major bottleneck in your organization. You're going to be spending some time and money, so make it something worth bragging about.

Phase 3: Vendor Independence

Up to this point, we have been adding blocks to the stack, and they were mostly smaller blocks representing add-on applications and modules. How about big blocks? Can we replace major, essential blocks from the single-vendor stack and replace them with other vendor applications?

There are few examples of organizations replacing fundamental modules of their single-vendor EHR with third-party equivalents. This last section of the phased unvendor project is therefore more hypothetical and more a set of potential directions than actual examples. We're going out on a limb with possible unvendor scenarios that may or may not be right for your organization but offer possibilities for various organizations.

Some health systems "inherit" a situation with large IT components from other vendors. Hospitals buy primary care or specialty practices with other EHRs. Health systems buy hospitals with other EHRs. Acquisitions and mergers often cause mixed EHR situations. These are resolved by forcing the acquired party to convert to the buyer's main EHR. And in most cases, that is the right move, for all the right reasons: organizational standardization, a single patient-facing portal, a consistent EHR experience for the clinical staff. But these mergers can also offer opportunities for maintaining a multivendor ecosystem and combining the best of both worlds.

AMBULATORY EHRS

In chapter 2, we discussed how some large EHR vendors became dominant by supporting inpatient acute care and ambulatory care with a single EHR. The slogan was "one patient, one record," and that was a good strategy. But with ongoing improvement of interoperability standards, it may not be the only strategy.

In the US today, there are four or five firms with an inpatient EHR but well more than one hundred firms with ambulatory EHRs. Many are small firms with niche EHRs. Some of the most successful ambulatory EHRs serve a specific medical specialty, such as dermatology, ophthalmology, or urology, fine-tuned to the need of that specific domain. Those users would not readily change to a "general purpose" ambulatory EHR.

This will require that you invest in interoperability. Create an efficient data exchange between the inpatient EHR and the (one or more) ambulatory EHRs. This data exchange doesn't mean that each EHR needs to share all data with all other EHRs. There are two considerations that define the preferred direction of data flow.

- There are more ambulatory patients than inpatients. According to the National Center for Health Statistics, each year approximately 5 percent of people have a hospital stay.[56] Don't make the mountain come to Moses—work to give inpatient providers access to ambulatory data and worry less about giving ambulatory providers access to inpatient data.

- Inpatient clinicians must have access to a patient's ambulatory history: their prior visit notes, medications, lab and imaging

---

56 National Center for Health Statistics, "Hospitalization—Health, United States," accessed November 12, 2024, https://www.cdc.gov/nchs/hus/topics/hospitalization.htm.

results. The reverse case is not as strong. In ambulatory care, a provider needs to see the patient's discharge summary, but inpatient medications, lab tests, radiology results, and other inpatient details are often not as important for the ongoing ambulatory care. And by law, each inpatient EHR already sends the discharge summary to the patient's PCP via a Secure Direct Message.

To make a mixed EHR ecosystem work, focus on giving the inpatient EHR users access to ambulatory records, both from the same-vendor EHR, as well as other-vendor EHRs. The region's HIE can be a starting point with already established data connections to other practices and their EHRs. CCD exchange for clinical documents may be a starting point—but they suffer from the CCD downsides we discussed earlier. The most up-to-date method would be FHIR queries for exactly those elements requested by the user.

We also should consider the patient as the conduit of the patient record. As Apple Health demonstrates, and other systems will likely follow, the patient can own and control a copy of their records, from multiple providers, and give permission to share and exchange. It has long been the vision of data exchange that the patient is the exchange hub, and we may be reaching a reality point in that vision.[57]

If your organization has a well-functioning, organization-wide EHR, then a single enterprise-wide EHR is the obvious solution. If, on the other hand, your organization does not have a well-established, highly functional EHR, with user frustrations and functional shortcomings, then it doesn't make sense to consolidate on that single

---

57   K. D. Mandl and I. S. Kohane, "Time for a Patient-Driven Health Information Economy?" *New England Journal of Medicine* 374 (2016): 205–8, https://doi.org/10.1056/NEJMp1512142.

EHR. A more diverse, interconnected solution may work better. Until something better comes along!

REVENUE CYCLE MANAGEMENT

In the panel discussion in chapter 4, I suggested that organizations might reduce IT spending by replacing modules from an expensive EHR system with a less expensive alternative. I'm unaware of any examples where organizations have actually done this, but it's certainly an option. The same caveat is true here: if your organization has a well-functioning comprehensive single-vendor system, this might not be a consideration. But other organizations may be less committed to their vendor partner and would consider a swap. RCM would be a target opportunity.

RCM users don't often cross paths with clinical and operational EHR users. It's possible to draw a line between the EHR and RCM components. In the best-of-breed era, it was common to have "financials" from one vendor and "clinicals" from another. But while there is not a lot of user crossover, data from the EHR side is critical for the RCM side to work. A solid data-exchange pipe is required to feed codes, charges, time stamps, and durations into the RCM module. Traffic will be mostly from EHR to RCM, not in the other direction.

Swapping out the RCM module may start as a head fake in the negotiation process with the EHR vendor. And it may end up being the right move.

ANALYTICS

As a "big block" in the stack, analytics is a promising and realistic option. Instead of looking at analytics as a block in the stack, it may be more appropriate to consider it as a separate stack altogether. A stack side by side with the operational health IT stack, recognizing that an analytics stack has a data layer, a data aggregation layer, one or more analytics tools and applications, AI modules, report production, visualization and dashboarding, and more. They can all be from one vendor, but it's also common to include third-party tools in the analytics stack.

An analytics stack for a health system will likely include data from outside the EHR, for example, claims data from payers, social determinants data from external sources, clinical data from partner organizations, patient satisfaction survey data, or data from third-party applications. A best-practice analytics stack would be a good choice if your organization is aggregating data from multiple sources.

Dr. Rasu Shrestha, introduced earlier, makes a strong case for a separate analytics environment: "If you're a health system that does research, that's a separate stack, and where appropriate there is a translation to the clinical and operational system, moving from a less controlled environment to a more tightly controlled environment."

Not every health system has the need or ability to invest in a separate analytics environment. It's a big investment in software, IT staff, ETL team, and data science staff. For research organizations and health systems with a large population health business, analytics is a primary use case that warrants strategic investment in a separate, state-of-the-art analytics environment.

Workbook

Creating a diverse IT stack with components from multiple vendors requires more than just software. Here is a list of organizational capabilities that you may need to start on the unvendoring path. Check those that you have in place today. Mark the other elements where you may need to grow or expand your organization's capacity.

ORGANIZATION ELEMENT	AVAILABLE? ATTAINABLE?
Strategic plan	
Executive support	
Culture of change and innovation	
IT team with interoperability skills	
Informatics team	
Funding/budget	
Change management team	
Innovation office	
User representation/committees	
Data governance committee	
Analytics/BI/data science team	
Others?	

Figure 11: Organization elements needed for unvendor projects

CHAPTER 8

STACKING UP ON ARTIFICIAL INTELLIGENCE AND MACHINE LEARNING

A I and ML information is everywhere. I don't need to review the basics, but I do want to talk about AI and ML in the context of your health IT stack and taking a smart and reasonable approach to bringing these technologies into your organization.

I have been intrigued with AI since I started my career in computer science and informatics. I read Edward Feigenbaum's *The Fifth Generation: Artificial Intelligence and Japan's Computer Challenge to the World*, and Alvin Toffler's *The Third Wave* about the knowledge- and information-based economy that seemed just around the corner. However, the promised wave and next generation did not happen. Now forty years later, AI and ML are here but not in the way these early thinkers predicted.

I tracked early expert systems in medicine, such as MYCIN, CADUCEUS, and others. They aimed to help physicians make better decisions, better diagnoses, better therapy plans. While the expert systems were strong, particularly on a narrow domain such as antibiotic therapy, they did not find widespread use among clinicians. I believe the main reason for the lack of uptake was that they solved problems that didn't need solving. Physicians were as good, or better, than the expert systems.

There is a critical distinction between these early expert systems and the current wave of AI/ML applications. Early systems had rule-based knowledge bases, engineered by subject-matter experts. The knowledge came from humans, formulated as a large web of if-then-else rules; for example, if HbA1C > 6.5 percent then the diagnosis is diabetes. Current AI and ML technology flips the script. The knowledge driving these systems is derived from data, not from humans—hence the term "machine learning." Deriving knowledge from data requires large amounts of data, preferably clean data. That fundamental requirement determines where AI solutions are available, and where they are not, or not yet. Without large data sets as ML stock, there can be no AI solutions.

It is how Oliver Wendell Holmes Jr. described law: "The life of the law has not been logic; it has been experience."[58] Today's AI is built on the experience of large data sets, not the logic of if-then-else statements.

AI today is not just a clinical DS tool. AI shows up as embedded technology in a wide variety of smart applications. Generative AI, the most common version of modern AI, also known as a large language model, and familiar to everyone who uses ChatGPT, Gemini (formerly Bard), or Copilot, is embedded into applications that deal with language: clinical documentation, message handling, or text-based patient engagement tools.

Let's look at some of the main application areas where AI is embedded. Large EHR firms have created integration points for some

---

58   Wikiquote, "Oliver Wendell Holmes Jr.," https://en.wikiquote.org/wiki/
       Oliver_Wendell_Holmes_Jr.

AI-based modules. These are all examples of unvendoring as add-on applications in the health IT stack.

AMBIENT DOCUMENTATION

Most of us are now familiar with large language model AI, also known as generative AI. It forms the foundation of ambient scribes that generate visit notes from dictation or ambient recording of the patient-provider dialogue, used in Abridge, DAX, Sunoh, and other note generators.

People have expressed concerns about AI replacing workers or making certain jobs obsolete. In the case of automated ambient note-taking, the reality is that it's increasing the efficiency of caregivers by automating one of the more mundane and time-consuming tasks. It doesn't make documentation entirely automatic, as providers still need to review the note and verify it is correct and complete.

AUTOMATED INBOX AND MESSAGE HANDLING

Providers get a lot of messages, from patients and from team members. We all suffer from message fatigue, and handling messages takes up a significant amount of clinician time, often leading to inefficiencies and staff burnout. Many messages are routine, and AI can help manage the inbox. EHR vendors use large language model AI models to help clinicians handle their messages efficiently.

SMART DEVICES

Stethoscopes, point-of-care ultrasound devices, heart-rhythm trackers, and CGM systems are all smart devices with AI algorithms built in. They record the signal, match it to a large set of known examples, and provide interpretation or recommendation. These smart devices challenge both the business model and care model by putting sophisticated diagnostic tools at the primary care front line.

COMPUTER VISION APPLICATIONS

There is a growing set of AI-assisted imaging and vision applications built around computer vision: image interpretation, fall detection, wound care tracking, and physical therapy tracking.

CLINICAL DECISION SUPPORT

Twenty-five years ago, I would have put CDS at the top of the list of AI applications. Clinical documentation and smart devices have a broader reach and a stronger potential for ROI, but CDS is still an important application area for AI. Scott Weingarten, the founder of Zynx Health, started the company built around sets of human-engineered CDS rules. His current firm, Stanson Health, uses AI to deliver DS in narrow, high-value domains, such as hierarchical condition category coding and reducing unnecessary and inappropriate care.[59] AI is strongest in narrow, specific domains where it can be trained on high-quality data sets, and that's the foundation for DS in these well-defined high-value use cases.

AI-SUPPORTED REFERRALS

VBC requires targeted and appropriate use of specialty care, with careful consideration on when a patient needs to see a specialist, what specialty is most appropriate, and what tests and information needs to be available prior to the specialist visit. Medpearl[60] is an AI-powered referral coach developed by Providence Health. Toyin Falola, vice

---

59   PINC AI, "Clinical Decision Support | Stanson Health," accessed November 12, 2024, https://www.pinc-ai.com/stanson-health/clinical-decision-support/.

60   MedPearl, 2024, https://www.medpearl.com/.

president of virtual care and digital health, explains how Medpearl combines AI with clinical DS, content management, and a no-code platform to insert recommendations into the referral workflow. Dr. Falola: "Medpearl-assisted referrals became very popular within the Providence system with over seven thousand physicians using it. Other health systems want to use it, so now we're spinning it out through our commercialization."

ORCHESTRATION AND WORKFLOW MANAGEMENT

Raj Toleti, Andor's CEO, sees an opportunity where the various AI capabilities feeding into the EHR, such as large language models and computer vision, will allow AI to "complement the orchestration." Orchestration in large health systems is very complex, involving many team players with independent schedules and workflows, and a reimbursement-driven urgency.

Orchestration is a close cousin to process automation, and here, too, AI-enabled tools are built into RPA and process management tools. UiPath calls it "process and task mining"—using AI to derive processes from operational data flows and using that data to improve the process. They coin the term "process intelligence" as a "combination of AI-rich capabilities built around a core of advanced process, task and communications mining."[61] Healthcare processes are complex, and at the same time are repetitive and predictable. Using AI

---

61   Chirag Dekate et al., "AI Operating Models for CXOs: Gartner® Report | UiPath," Gartner® Report: "Quick Answer: How Should CXOs Structure AI Operating Models?" February 2023, https://www.uipath.com/resources/automation-analyst-reports/ai-operating-models-for-cxos-gartner-report?utm_source=google&utm_medium=paid_search&utm_team=pdi&utm_team_geo=global&utm_campaign=US_Tier-1_ENG_Brand_T2_Product&utm_term=uipath%20ai-p-c-g&utm_content=B_Product-AI-Center&gad_source=1&gclid=Cj0KCQiA5 7G5BhDUARIsACgCYnzbYZpDBlyMo-NoaW_M1PH3G-X95FSot3btzpgm4rzB1cK-b5LGHnRUaAmFkEALw_wcB&gclsrc=aw.ds.

tools to gain insight into workflow processes and then building team orchestration will be a major role for embedded AI tools.

ANALYTICS

Kyle Armstrong, fellow lecturer at Thomas Jefferson University and senior data scientist at Temple University in Philadelphia, Pennsylvania, explains the layers of AI and ML in an analytics stack: "AI is the broad set of any type of automation in data processing. ML is a subset of AI and includes traditional statistical models such as linear and logistic regression but also more complex models like random forest, naive Bayes, and k-nearest neighbors. Deep learning (DL) is a further subset of ML and uses artificial neural networks. Generative deep-learning models such as ChatGPT are now gaining adoption in healthcare research."

How will users know what tool is most useful for their data analysis? Armstrong: "The choice of methods depends on the amount of available data, the complexity of the research question, the time and resources allocated to the project, and the end goals of the analysis. An analytics project then becomes an iterative process, starting with basic univariate and multivariate regression, preparing for ML models and then proceeding to deep learning pipelines."

As in other applications, the AI tools in analytics are embedded in the overall environment. In analytics, however, the analyst, as end user, is more in control of how and when to apply specific AI technologies. Many health data analysts will need training and experience in the use of AI methodologies to make effective use of these tools.

■　■　■

AI-enabled applications will come from a broad number of software vendors. One company or vendor cannot create all AI modules needed in an organization. Vendors may have "over 100 AI projects underway,"[62] but it's unrealistic to believe that they will all be successful. We should expect that AI modules will come from a number of niche, high-tech, specialized firms.

AI will be embedded into documentation tools, diagnostic devices, radiology systems, process automation systems, and data analytics tools, specifically designed for the task. Rather than health IT teams building or configuring organization-specific AI, they will purchase and install AI-enabled applications.

AI and ML applications in healthcare are brand new and will continue to evolve quickly. I see three ways in which CIOs and CMIOs need to lead their organizations in AI adoption:

Curation. AI-powered applications come from your EHR vendor as well as a variety of third-party vendors. Your team's role is curation, deciding which applications to acquire and implement, and tracking the success of these applications. Curation is a two-way process: in and out. You may bring in an orchestration or documentation tool, and in four years the technology will have evolved, requiring replacement with a newer, stronger alternative. That's okay—the point of unvendoring is not keeping a tool ten years or more. Remember, we're going for flexibility, and the AI space calls for such as technology continues to evolve and improve.

Curation is ongoing: add more as you go. Don't aim for permanence but evaluate and replace if needed. Especially in a dynamic and fast-moving space as AI and ML, curation allows you to swap tools in and out as tools evolve and as the organization matures.

---

62   Ashley Capoot, "Epic Systems Is Building More Than 100 New AI Features for Doctors and Patients. Here's What's Coming," CNBC, August 21, 2024, https://www.cnbc.com/2024/08/21/epic-systems-ugm-2024-ai-tools-in-mychart-cosmos-.html.

Adoption and understanding. AI is ubiquitous in social media: we all see AI-generated content, from search results to fake news. We need to become smart consumers, recognizing what is real, what is fake, and what our role is as information consumers. The same is true for healthcare users. If you use an AI-assisted scribe, review the document to ensure it's accurate, complete, and actionable to your fellow clinicians and to the patient. If you use AI-powered analytics, review findings and recommendations to ensure they are in line with expectations. Users need to understand the power as well as the limitations of the tools. It's the role of IT leaders to educate an organization's users in the appropriate use of AI-powered applications.

Aligning care model and business model. In chapter 2, we saw how healthcare is at the intersection of care, reimbursement, and technology. The introduction of AI applications is a great example of a disruptive technology impacting the care model and, even more so, the business model. Point-of-care devices may reduce revenue from imaging departments and specialist referrals. AI-assisted coding will change the staffing needs of the HIM department. AI-assisted documentation and message handling will reduce the EHR burden for clinicians, giving them more time with patients or allowing them to see more patients. Smart stethoscopes can help avoid hospitalizations or ED visits. Many health systems still rely heavily on fee-for-service payments, and these technologies present a threat to the bottom line. That will not stop the advance of AI-powered applications. As we transition slowly to VBC and at-risk payments, these technologies will support the new business model.

AI-enabled applications are perfect examples of unvendor projects. They can occur almost anywhere in the stack. They can sit on top or next to or inside your existing EHR, requiring data exchange and interoperability into the user's workflow. AI-powered applications drive innovation in the clinical and business side of healthcare delivery. Let's explore this more in the workbook.

Workbook

Let's start with an easy question: Where in the application stack do we expect AI applications?

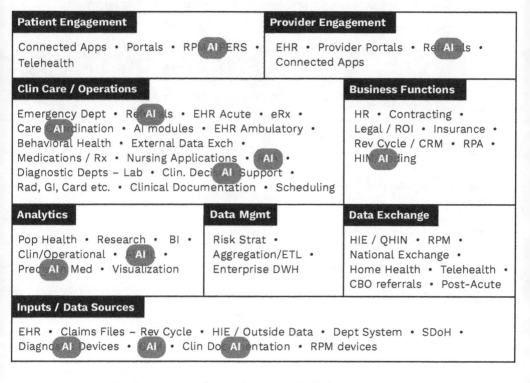

Figure 12: Stack components that can have AI embedded

Figure 12 shows how AI can be embedded in many applications and show up at every level of the applications stack. You can match the applications that are marked with AI with the examples in the chapter. Are there more applications where you see AI built in?

Curating AI-powered applications is an important role for the IT and informatics teams. There are many factors to consider when deciding where to introduce AI, where to go next, and what the priorities are. Use the table below to estimate both the effort required to bring this capability into your organization, and its impact. Based on effort and impact, can you outline in what order you would introduce these applications? There is room at the bottom to add additional application spaces. Use high/medium/low for effort and impact estimates.

AI-embedded application	Effort	IMPACT					PRIORITY
		Care Quality	Care Efficiency	User Exp.	Patient Exp.	ROI/ VOI	
Clinical documentation		H	H	H			
Message handling							
Smart diagnostic devices							
Computer vision							
Clinical DS							
Orchestration							
Analytics							
Remote monitoring							
Referrals							
Other:							

Figure 13: Prioritize AI applications for your organization.

One last question in this workbook. In a population health/VBC practice, patient-level AI tools can improve the practice's performance, one patient at a time. Organization-level tools can help at a practice or health system level: How does an organization improve its clinical and financial performance in the VBC setting?

How do you want AI/ML to assist in the implementation and optimization of your population health and VBC strategy?

Patient level:

- Risk stratification

- Care coordination

- Care plans

- Patient engagement

- Quality measures

Organization level:

- Contracting analytics and strategy

- Provider performance analysis and optimization

- Care management analysis and strategy

Depending on which areas you selected, do you think the AI tool has sufficient data to train and to determine which strategies are most likely to improve the practice's performance?

PART FOUR

WHAT'S NEXT

I nformation systems are critical healthcare infrastructure. They determine how we care for patients, communication with team members, and how we run our organizations. We are the stewards of this healthcare nervous system, and it's important that we look ahead and prepare for what's next.

Depending on your appetite for disruption, there are two ways to look at what's coming next. One way is to be prepared for upcoming changes. Be ready for the moment in ten years or so when some large vendors may not be around, or not in their current capacity.

The other way is to *make* the future happen by actively moving your health system beyond the current state.

Be prepared for change. Or drive the change.

In these final chapters, I will make the case that option two, driving the change, is not only the best strategy for your healthcare organization but also for health IT vendors. In the long run, they can't be all things to all people as a single do-it-all monolithic stack. The future path is to become a platform, an underlying technology allowing other technologies to ride on top. IT vendors need their clients and customers to use the EHR as a platform for other technologies, at all layers of the stack. In the long run, unvendoring will preserve the core functions of EHR vendors. I believe some large vendors know this and are preparing their own organizations and clients for this future state.

Before we consider what this future state may look like, we first need to stare into the abyss and see how large IT companies potentially fail. From there, we'll chart the path to the health IT platform of the future.

CHAPTER 9

HOW DO MEGAVENDORS FAIL?

There is no shortage of large companies failing to anticipate a technological innovation or business disruption and then disappear from the market. Blockbuster was wiped out by Netflix and their DVDs in the mail model and then by streaming. Kodak became obsolete following the switch from film to digital photography. Sears department stores were made irrelevant by online shopping and e-commerce. In hindsight these failures seem obvious, predictable, and possibly preventable if the company had anticipated the shift in technology, but that's often not how it goes. They don't see the wave coming until it's too late.

Blackberry stands out in my memory. I'm of the Blackberry generation. Everyone in my firm had one and was on it day in, day out. We called them "crackberries." The Blackberry was the precursor to the smartphone, and the smartphone was the asteroid that killed this dinosaur. Why didn't Blackberry anticipate this newer technology and keep their devices up to date? Why didn't they realize there was a market for mobile devices outside the corporate world?

The story behind these large failures starts with a technology shift, with new players emerging suddenly, shifting the market, causing bankruptcy and obsolescence. The companies fail, but clients and consumers end up with a better product and improved service. The world moves on.

Health IT has similar stories of success and failure. We can look at the past and try to understand the future. Let's review a few case studies.

Case Studies

SMS–SIEMENS–CERNER–ORACLE HEALTH

I spent the first ten years of my health IT career at SMS, Shared Medical Systems, in Malvern, Pennsylvania. It was a young company with innovative technology to run hospital administration and billing from a shared data center. SMS was heavily invested in mainframe computing and struggled to make the transition to modern client/ server technology. The German technology giant Siemens acquired SMS in 2000 in a bid to combine medical diagnostic equipment (imaging, lab instruments, monitors) with an IT backbone. The Siemens team, with global ambitions, built the EHR from the ground up on modern technology, under the brand name Soarian. Things went well until they didn't, and in 2015 Cerner bought Siemens Health Services. Unfortunately for Cerner, most Siemens clients switched to Epic. In 2022, Oracle acquired Cerner and now operates under the Oracle Health brand.

You might say these were acquisitions, not failures. Yes, but under the covers, they were failures. These were not strategic takeovers but rather opportunistic rescues, and in each cycle, the resulting team was weaker, not stronger.

Technology played a role: the failure to switch from mainframe technology to client-server architecture set SMS back. Siemens's inability to build a new EHR in a short time frame caused many clients to leave.

The main failure, however, was a market change. SMS, Siemens, and Cerner all maintained separate systems for hospital and ambulatory use, and these systems didn't connect well. Epic introduced the single EHR for ambulatory and acute care, just as healthcare providers consolidated hospitals and outpatient practices within one organization. These integrated delivery systems insisted on a single record for their patients. At the root of the SMS/Siemens/Cerner failure is missing the market demand for a single patient record.

The result of this chain of acquisitions is Oracle Health, one of the current health IT megavendors. Out of these ashes emerges a possible new EHR. In late 2024, Oracle Health announced that they will release a new AI-powered EHR with a user interface driven by speech rather than menus and clicks. Seema Verma, executive vice president and general manager of Oracle Health and Life Sciences, calls it a disruptive system. It would be a welcome addition to an otherwise stagnant market.

Risk factors: technology shift, missed care model and market demand shift, multiple leadership changes

MCKESSON HBOC

This case study is an example of a direct path to failure. In the 1980s, HBOC was one of the two largest players in health IT. McKesson, a pharmaceutical and medical equipment distribution company, acquired HBOC in 1999. Prior to this merger, HBOC fraudulently inflated its revenue through improper accounting practices. The scandal caused a significant drop in McKesson's stock price, damaged the company's reputation, and led to the failure of the health IT division.

Risk factors: business practices, missed market demand shift

TECHNICON DATA SYSTEMS–ECLIPSYS– ALLSCRIPTS–HARRIS HEALTHCARE–ALTERA

Technicon Data Systems was a leading health IT company in the 1970s and 1980s. Their claim to fame was that they were the first system where physicians entered orders for tests and medications directly into the computer using computerized provider order entry (CPOE). In fact, this process was considered the litmus test for EHR usability. Eclipsys acquired Technicon Data Systems and marketed the system under the Sunrise brand, one of the most popular and successful EHRs of the time.

However, the company struggled with the challenges of maintaining and updating the EHR in the face of rapidly advancing technology and changing market demands. The need for an integrated ambulatory and acute care EHR caused the market to move away from Eclipsys. In 2010, Allscripts, an ambulatory EHR company, merged with Eclipsys, hoping that the combination would offer an integrated solution. Allscripts's market share both in the acute and ambulatory markets continues to decline. Allscripts was acquired by Harris Healthcare in 2022, and the firm now sells EHR software under the Altera brand.

There is another contributing factor in this story: failure to integrate software from multiple companies into a single EHR system. Each party brings a technology inheritance and an existing client base. To be successful, the firm would need to convert their entire installed client base to the new platform. I am not aware of a single case where the integration of two systems resulted in a successful EHR. Instead of selling a single strong product, it looks like a yard sale.

Risk factors: technology shift, missed care model and market demand shift, inability to integrate products

Risks and Opportunities

Health IT is a difficult space. Clinical users are highly educated, highly demanding, often overworked, and looking for tools to streamline efficiency. EHRs can look dated compared to the consumer software they are used to, and instead of making them more efficient, the EHR slows down their work and adds to the workload. Healthcare organizations are generally conservative and slow in decision-making, making sales cycles long and tedious.

Despite all that, a handful of very successful firms have dominated this market for many years. Epic is at the top of the KLAS Research "Best in KLAS" list year after year. They were the first with a "one patient, one record" concept with an EHR that supports ambulatory and acute care in a single system. While Epic is at the high end of the price range, Meditech provides a very similar integrated EHR at the "economy" end of the market scale. Oracle Health is also still a major player with potential for long-term success.

What are the risks and opportunities facing these firms?

Throughout this book, I have mostly avoided mentioning specific EHRs or EHR firms. I believe the unvendor strategy is valid no matter what EHR your organization uses. This next section mentions EHR firms and their potential risk factors. Of course, writing future case studies is speculative, but let's look at several scenarios that might change our EHR landscape over the next five to ten years.

EPIC SYSTEMS

In the Bible's Book of Daniel, King Nebuchadnezzar of Babylon has a dream of a giant statue with a head of gold and feet made of clay. Daniel explains to the king that the statue represents successive kingdoms, with the clay feet representing a weak foundation for current society. If we live in an Epic Systems kingdom, what are the clay feet we need to be concerned about?

Technology shift. Epic's software is written in MUMPS, an arcane healthcare-specific programming language. This hasn't slowed the company down from becoming the largest player in health IT, but it's still a cause for concern. Agile competitors with modern software and access to software engineers with general-use programming languages can introduce innovations quickly, and might surpass Epic in terms of performance, cost-effectiveness, and scalability. Epic supports standard FHIR APIs and HL7 interfacing, allowing modern applications to integrate with the Epic system. This is the foundation for unvendor projects. These APIs can protect the core software and allow modern software extensions to keep up with new technologies.

Market shift. Epic's business model depends heavily on large hospitals and healthcare systems. If there is a shift in healthcare delivery models toward outpatient care, telehealth, and VBC, Epic may struggle to adjust its offerings to smaller providers. This shift could make their current high-cost, complex systems less relevant in an evolving healthcare landscape that values lower-cost, nimble solutions for a dispersed provider network.

Economic headwinds or cost sensitivity. Epic is known for its high implementation and maintenance costs. If healthcare providers face financial pressures due to an economic downturn or reimbursement reductions, they may look for more affordable EHR solutions. Changing the business model is a driver for unvendoring. Epic's lack of price flexibility can make it difficult to retain clients in a more cost-sensitive environment.

Culture and leadership challenges. Judy Faulkner started the firm in her basement and grew it to the multibillion firm it is today. She is a phenomenal leader in the health IT industry, with a personality and style that define the firm's culture. Product names, building designs, customer events, HR policies, and most importantly health IT strategy all bear Faulkner's personal design and direction. If leadership transitions poorly after Faulkner's retirement, it could lose its competitive edge. An inability to foster new leadership that understands future trends could lead to missed opportunities and eventual decline.

Any of these factors can be the clay feet of the giant, the cause for a downturn or change in direction for Epic and their customers. The large and powerful health systems making up Epic's client base will play a major role in deciding the future for Epic, and the future for health IT in general. They can, collectively, make the change happen and steer the industry in the right direction.

ORACLE HEALTH

As leaders in health IT, you have likely played roles in many hospitals and health systems. Has it occurred to you that when walking through hospitals, some hallways slope slightly uphill or down? Or awkwardly bend left or right? Most hospitals have grown over time, with new buildings added along the way and older buildings connected to each other. The sloping and crooked hallways are telltales of expansion projects.

That's a bit like Oracle Health. Where Epic's software system is entirely Epic-built, without any acquisitions or mergers, Oracle Health consists of acquisitions and software integrations. Having a software base from multiple sources and origins makes it more difficult to support, troubleshoot, and continue to develop and innovate.

What might be the risk factors for Oracle Health?

Integration challenges. Integrating Cerner and its subsystems into Oracle, if it succeeds, will be a spectacular move in health IT, bringing healthcare software inside a true enterprise software corporation. It also carries a risk. Mergers and acquisitions come with integration challenges. It's not just a software integration project. Customer integration adds to the complexity: if Oracle can't leverage cloud capabilities and enterprise software in its new health space, it can lead to customer dissatisfaction and further loss of market share.

VA contract perils. In 2018, Cerner won the contract with the US Department of Veterans Affairs to replace the Veterans Affairs homegrown EHR at all its facilities. It's an enormous contract, and it hasn't gone well. In 2023, Cerner and Veterans Affairs renegotiated contract terms and paused further deployment. Failure to deliver on this contract would not only be a financial loss but could severely damage Oracle Health's reputation and impact its ability to secure future government and commercial contracts.

Client-base shift. There is a multiyear shift in Oracle Health's client base. Larger hospitals and health systems leave Oracle Health and switch to Epic. Smaller hospitals continue with Oracle Health.[63] As this trend continues, Oracle Health finds itself serving a segment of the market with lower profit margins, less ability to support complicated IT projects, and a generally weaker client base. While Oracle Health is seeking to scale up its clients and bring them to enterprise-level software, the client base goes in the other direction, to smaller hospitals, critical access hospitals, and a suboptimal market for high-end sophisticated software.

---

63   Paul Warburton and Tyson Blauer, "Current Trends in US Hospital EMR
       Market Share," KLAS Research, June 2023, https://klasresearch.com/article/
       current-trends-in-us-hospital-emr-market-share/1022.

Inability to meet regulatory and interoperability requirements. These regulatory requirements apply to all EHR firms, but it will be more difficult for Oracle Health to meet them across their multiple software platforms. The trend toward smaller hospital clients with limited capacity for software implementations and upgrades adds to the challenge. This is not optional. If Oracle Health's systems are seen as noncompliant with new regulations, healthcare providers may switch to competitors that are better able to keep up with regulatory standards.

Oracle Health seems to be in a perfect storm of challenges. Cerner was already struggling with its Veterans Affairs contract and client defections prior to the Oracle Health acquisition. The Oracle merger may aggravate and accelerate these troubles. But an optimistic observer would see the opportunities here: by merging with Oracle, Cerner can rise to a level of enterprise software sophistication and ultimately rise above these challenges. It will be worth watching this case study as it moves to the next stage with the development and introduction of a new AI-powered EHR in the coming years.

MEDITECH

Meditech is a long-standing EHR firm and is known for its stability and focus on serving midsized and smaller hospitals. In that sense, it's not as exposed to the same market turmoil that faces Oracle Health. But while it continues to do well in its preferred market space, there are long-term challenges.

Technology shift. Like Epic, Meditech's platform is built on the MUMPS programming language, and it has been slower to adopt cutting-edge technologies compared to its competitors. Meditech lags in integrating AI, cloud computing, and other modern technologies into its products. Because of the focus on smaller and midsized health-care clients, it may not be able to invest in the kind of research and

173

development needed to stay competitive with larger, more resource-rich companies.

Poor UX and client dissatisfaction. Meditech's clients have become increasingly dissatisfied with the UX, struggling with issues such as complexity, lack of user-friendly interfaces, and workflow inefficiencies. If these usability issues persist or worsen, they could drive customers away, especially with the focus on reducing clinician EHR burden.

ATHENAHEALTH AND ECLINICALWORKS

There are more than a hundred EHR firms in the ambulatory care space, making it a very fragmented market. These two firms are the market share leaders as ambulatory-only vendors. They have something else in common: both firms were very close to entering the acute care market by adding inpatient functionality. They both were on the verge of going live in one or more US hospitals, but for various reasons weren't able to scale that high mountain to a viable acute care solution. That's disappointing because the US EHR market would be more dynamic and competitive with additional choices and price points for provider organizations.

The threat to all ambulatory-only EHR vendors is the consolidation of healthcare provider organizations into large integrated health networks, which implement a single EHR across all providers. This consolidation trend drives more practices toward EHRs run by large health systems and limits the potential market share for ambulatory vendors.

Ambulatory EHR firms have certain advantages that keep them afloat and viable. They are far less expensive on a per-provider basis than large-vendor EHRs. The implementation effort and time to go live is usually very fast, even within six weeks in some cases, compared to months or years on large organization EHRs.

And there is an unvendor opportunity here. If a health system wants to reduce spending on their EHR megavendor, they can switch some or all ambulatory practices to a low-cost ambulatory EHR, while keeping the hospitals on the large EHR. With proper interoperability, focused on data exchange and workflow integration, a health system might carve out the ambulatory space to a different EHR system.

In short, the risks also create opportunities in mitigating circumstances to keep the ambulatory-only EHR players in the game.

Strategic Preparedness

There are common themes in these risk factors. Technology obsolescence is the most likely driver for any firm to fail, not just in health IT. Market shifts have caused some firms to succeed, and others to miss the opportunity and never catch up. Leadership and culture may not be visible to the outside world but are crucial to the long-term success and failure of any large firm.

Health IT is a difficult and slow-moving space. EHR contracts typically have ten-year terms and can be extended multiple times. Implementations and system conversions are slow and labor-intensive. This slow market allows underperforming firms to survive for many years. It also makes it more difficult for newcomers to enter and establish a foothold. While consumer technology changes fast, health IT is on a slower train.

In that sense, there is no imminent risk that your EHR vendor will suddenly be out of business or unable to provide services. I don't see a need to be prepared for EHR collapse. Instead, consider unvendor projects as strategic innovation with a side of risk mitigation. The primary motivator is flexibility, competitiveness, and possibly ROI. In addition, you're preparing your organization to be able to move if that becomes necessary. Call it strategic preparedness—execute health IT strategy with resilience as a secondary benefit.

And I'll take this one step further: not only can unvendoring isolate your organization from a future fail, but you may actually increase the long-term outlook for your EHR vendor. Unvendor projects will focus the EHR on the functions it does best, and should be doing, and become a platform for other applications to extend that functionality. The next chapter will discuss how clients can help direct their EHR vendors from "do everything" mode to "platform" mode. The give-and-take between client and vendor is critical for the vendor to reach the next level in software business maturity, and to serve as a platform rather than a monolithic system.

Workbook

Risk factors. In the diagram below, circle the potential risk factors for your EHR vendor. Which one is of greatest concern to you? Add any other factors to the diagram if you consider them relevant to the future of your EHR vendor as the provider of critical infrastructure to your organization.

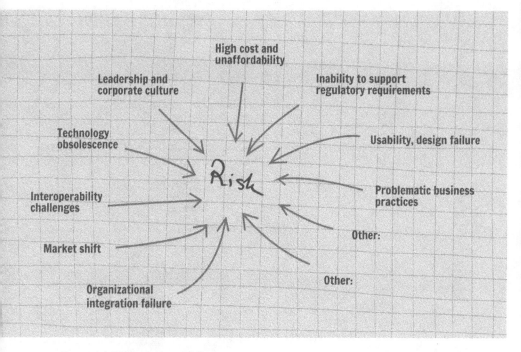

Figure 14: EHR vendor risk factors

MOVING TO PLATFORM

This next question sets us up for the platform discussion in chapter 10. If we're going to focus the EHR on EHR-essential functions and bring in third-party applications for functions that are outside the EHR essentials, where would we draw the line? In the grid below, can you create a box so EHR-essential functions are in the box, and potential unvendor applications are outside the box? Can you imagine how this design allows the EHR to focus on essential functions, and become a platform serving data and transactions to add-on applications?

Draw some arrows from inside the box to outside the box, and vice versa. What would the arrows represent? Do they align with

FHIR resources and APIs? Can you see the emergence of a platform architecture?

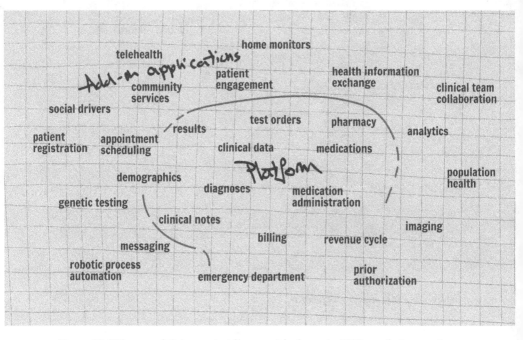

Figure 15: What capabilities are inside or outside the main EHR vendor's system?

CHAPTER 10

UNVENDOR HEALTHCARE

I n March of 1979, I was an exchange student in the small town of Corunna, Michigan. I remember the news of that month, the partial meltdown of Unit 2, one of the nuclear reactors at Three Mile Island in Harrisburg, Pennsylvania. President Carter meeting with the engineers to prevent a major disaster. Three Mile Island Unit 1 was shut down in 2019 because it could not compete with natural gas power plants.

Fast-forward to 2024. Microsoft just announced a deal with the owner of the Three Mile Island nuclear facility to restart Unit 1 to generate power for its data centers. Amazon just located one of its data centers near the Susquehanna nuclear power plant, also in Pennsylvania.[64]

Computing power is accelerating so fast that it requires nuclear plants to power them. I won't go into the pros and cons of nuclear power versus solar and wind, but the message is: this is big, and there is much, much more to come. We're not at a plateau in IT and data science; we're at Level 1 and preparing to power to the next levels. I

---

64   C. Crownhart, "Why Microsoft Made a Deal to Help Restart Three Mile Island," *MIT Technology Review*, September 2024, https://www.technologyreview.com/2024/09/26/1104516/three-mile-island-microsoft/.

want health IT to be a big part of that growth. We need to be part of this, and to do that, we need to bring in every bit of meaningful, powerful, impactful technology.

What would nuclear-powered computing mean for healthcare?

I'm visualizing a "Tesla/SpaceX hospital." Microphones in all locations, transcribing and documenting, in any language, for clinical notes, but also explaining the next steps to patients and families. Cameras everywhere, tracking equipment, medications, and keeping patients safe. AI technology not only transcribing notes, but tracking clinical and operational metrics, making staffing adjustments, optimizing schedules, balancing workloads. Precision medicine with precision care delivery. Imagine a self-driving hospital: efficient, safe, pleasant (for staff and for patients), and yes, high-tech, slick, and cool.

On the other hand, maybe we should invest nuclear power not in building up the acute care sector but expanding and strengthening the place where most people and patients are: in ambulatory care, and at home with their families. Not Tesla/SpaceX but Amazon/Uber: technology delivering high-tech, high-touch healthcare to consumers, on demand, at their location, without requiring expensive acute care centers. AI-powered algorithms and sensors for coaching, and as-needed support by caregivers and health professionals. A tech platform for public health and consumer-focused care will have a far greater impact and ROI than continued spending on acute care.

This is not an either/or question, and the answer is both. The health tech stack will get taller for the acute care organizations, and broader and wider for the consumer and public health space. In both settings, a diverse health stack with innovative applications, connected via a data and workflow backbone, can move healthcare toward high-tech and consumer service at the same time.

Dr. Rasu Shrestha compares an innovation project to a speedboat, versus the EHR vendor ocean liner: "You need a level of agility and nimbleness, a controlled set of speedboats. You can't have twenty random speedboats going around the harbor, that's uncoordinated and unorchestrated. The speedboats need to align around your specific strategies and priorities. Creating a carefully curated ecosystem is important."

Evolve Your Team

Dr. Toyin Falola, introduced earlier, worked for years in the start-up world, with venture-backed, publicly traded companies. Her role is product strategy: What shall we make, how shall we make it, and why would people want to use it? She's now in a similar role at Providence, evaluating new technologies and applications to develop and incubate their own solutions to spin off into the market.

Her world is a dichotomy of the start-up world (move fast and break things) and a health system (go slow and cautious). She says: "There is a lot that start-ups can learn from health systems about the diligence, the emphasis on privacy and security of data, but health systems need to think about the way start-ups work, which is faster go/no-go decision-making, iterative product development cycles, and try and test some ideas. Sometimes we diligence things to death, and we think too much about the tech stack that we already have, so that limits the technology that we're able to bring in. There are so many great technologies and ideas that may not be within the Epic or Microsoft portfolio." With that statement, Dr. Falola articulated the unvendor culture challenge of shifting a health system mindset toward a start-up mindset.

She explains how Providence's informatics team embraces the start-up approach: "One Providence superpower is thinking about what informatics is for the future. Historically, people think informatics is Epic or Oracle; it's getting the EHR to work. I think of informatics as: How do we handle data and analytics, how do we think about the workflow, and about the engineering? It's a forward-thinking multidisciplinary team of informaticians. They think not just about the EHR but about data movement, technology, and workflow."

It's not enough to change the mindset; we also need to change the skill set. IT and informatics teams need expertise in interoperability, FHIR API configuration and implementation, data aggregation and ETL, AI/ML applications, RPA tools, and more. Members of the informatics team in end-user-facing roles need to understand user preferences and options outside of the single EHR, and that will take time. My hope is that your team will not be split into an EHR faction and an everything-else faction, but rather, as much as possible, cross-train EHR specialists to also support third-party applications.

Prepare to unvendor by expanding the scope of your IT and informatics team. In Dr. Falola's words: "If you can reimagine what innovation is and informatics is, then your own clinicians and your own engineers can be doing this kind of stuff."

Evolve to a Platform for Healthcare Reform

Zeev Neuwirth is the author of *Beyond the Walls*, in which he describes how market disruptors transform the American healthcare landscape, and the success of platforms in creating two-sided, low-friction architectures. Platforms allow producers and consumers to connect, interact, engage, buy, and sell. Platforms also create an open architecture allowing other vendors and parties to participate. Examples of platforms are Amazon's marketplace, or Uber's and Lyft's transportation marketplaces. I asked Zeev whether he sees the large IT vendors becoming platform-like, and if he sees them transform themselves into connection and collaboration layers. "No, I don't see Epic or Oracle Health working as platforms today—which is why I didn't mention them as disruptors. They may be the ones needing to be disrupted."[65] EHRs "are stored and shared digitally, but they are used in a very channeled and linear one-to-one manner. That's totally unlike a platform ... which provide consumer-grade transparency, options, and ease of use." He adds, "How similar is your provider's or hospital's patient portal to Amazon's streaming entertainment experience? Not very."

I believe that some of the large health IT vendors' strategy is to become a platform. Where today they are mostly an enclosed system, a full suite of applications and proprietary data, it's quite possible that a move toward a true platform offers a path to relevance many years in the future. To do that, they need to become a two-sided open system: a data and transaction platform allowing partner firms to tap into the flow and interact with users using the application of their choice.

The vendors understand this and want to become a platform. Epic's Judy Faulkner says: "Epic is developing a platform that will better enable cooperation and data exchange between providers and payers."[66] Oracle Health's Seema Verma describes their platform strategy: "Another critical area is openness and interoperability. We always planned to be EHR-agnostic because part of the challenge today is that solutions sit in silos, making it difficult if not impossible

65   Zeev Neuwirth, *Beyond the Walls* (Advantage Books, 2023).

66   G. Bruce, "Judy Faulkner's 25-to-50-Year Plan for Epic," August 2024, https://www. beckershospitalreview.com/ehrs/judy-faulkners-25-to-50-year-plan-for-epic.html.

to connect the data that will fuel population health improvements, personalized medicine, disease prevention, and more. We believe in the power of the ecosystem, and we want to work with everyone."[67]

The move from monolithic stack to platform would be a perfect route to unvendoring, as a vendor-client partnership with future benefits to both parties. For some of the current EHR vendors, I see this as a path to the future, regaining competitive advantage and avoiding obsolescence in the long run.

Former White House CTO Aneesh Chopra, who was one of the designers of the HITECH program that gave us Meaningful Use (see chapter 2), refers to the original intent of the program: adopt a "health-care-centric" approach, focusing on population health improvement goals, and avoid a "technology-centric" approach focused on health IT adoption. The goal is not pure computerization, but computer-aided care and payment transformation.[68]

I asked Chopra about unvendoring the IT stack. He says: "Unvendoring is another word for enabling modular, nimble application development. I might call that the great decoupling—we decouple the data infrastructure from the application layer. For example, in any health system today, ask a doctor, is this patient in front of you in an ACO, and what new information do you get about the ACO patient versus a patient who is not in an ACO panel. They are likely to tell

> **Unvendoring is another word for enabling modular, nimble application development.**

---

67   Margaret Lindquist, "Oracle's Seema Verma on the Huge Opportunities in Healthcare and Life Sciences," February 2, 2024, https://www.oracle.com/health/seema-verma-interview/.

68   T. Park and P. Basch, "A Historic Opportunity—Wedding Health Information Technology to Care Delivery Innovation and Provider Payment Reform," May 2009, https://cdn.americanprogress.org/wp-content/uploads/issues/2009/05/pdf/health_it_execsumm.pdf.

you that they were the same. That tells you that we have failed in VBC delivery. And it tells you that the CIO has failed the institution for not supporting the new care model."

Both Chopra and Neuwirth see the necessity of disruptors in healthcare, and consequently in health IT. Neuwirth sees the need for a health IT platform rather than a monolithic EHR. Chopra calls it the great decoupling. It is the move toward a diverse health IT stack, enabling new care models and reimbursement models.

Evolve to Support the Healthcare Consumer

Jane Sarasohn-Kahn is a health economist, market watcher, futurist, and blogger at Health Populi.[69] She advises clients about the future of healthcare using scenario planning and environmental and health policy analysis. We meet regularly to discuss trends in health IT and how patients have evolved into healthcare consumers.

Sarasohn-Kahn points to the growing "retailization" of healthcare, with consumers paying more out of pocket, as a deductible or coinsurance. This creates a growing responsibility for the consumer as a payer, with fiduciary responsibility to spend money wisely and to exercise the power of the consumer in choosing their providers, their care team, and their preferred method of taking care of their health.

Much of consumer healthcare delivery revolves around IT. She monitors the large consumer health tech companies: "We're seeing home monitoring technologies coming out of South Korea, driven by Samsung's ecosystem. Samsung is wiring the home as the health

---

69 J. Sarasohn-Kahn, "Most People in the US Trust the CDC and NIH for Health Information, and Most Want President Trump to Strengthen Health Institutions," Health Populi, https://www.healthpopuli.com/.

hub, the smart bathroom, the smart kitchen, the smart bedroom. And include Apple and Amazon as healthcare ecosystem firms, like Samsung, they are in healthcare for the long game." She's signaling a shift where the EHR may not be the center of healthcare delivery, and another center is forming around the home and the consumer.

Focusing on consumer needs should be an essential component of VBC. According to a *JAMA Viewpoint* article, "If the United States intends to pay on the basis of value, it is essential to ask patients what they value, and then deliver on those priorities."[70] That means not only measuring care through HbA1C levels, but also documenting patients' priorities, including on "receiving treatment at home, having a trustworthy care-system that is always available, and reducing challenges facing family caregivers." This, too, represents a shift away from the EHR-centric data system to a more inclusive data set that evolves around the consumers and their technology platforms.

Let's emphasize again that the EHR and the consumer health technologies need to be connected spaces to deliver the care experience that patients seek. This is the essence of the platform: the ability for a diverse set of technologies to tap into the EHR's health data backbone. It's about extending the health IT stack into the patient and consumer space. Only a multivendor ecosystem can deliver on that promise.

Exercise Your Power as a Health IT Consumer

I did not write this book with the intention of being contrarian or provocative. I realize there are many advantages to a single-vendor stack, and that many healthcare organizations thrive on their single,

---

70   J. Lynn et al., "Value-Based Payments Require Valuing What Matters to Patients," *JAMA* 314, no. 14 (2015), https://doi.org/10.1001/jama.2015.8909.

integrated system. But I'm hoping that this book will have inspired you to swing the pendulum, even a little bit, back to a more innovative, flexible IT ecosystem. I want to encourage you and your team to become more progressive and diverse in your IT strategy. Aneesh Chopra gets that: "To me, the story of unvendoring is the story of CIOs who understand current and future demand of information and insights to do a job. It's having modular app ecosystems, and data infrastructure, that give us the flexibility to respond to needs."

Many small, innovative start-up firms build applications around AI. Bring them into our organizations and let your clinicians and healthcare workers experience these new tools and applications. Take a page from Providence Health's examples in incorporating a start-up mentality into the organization. Many other health systems embrace innovation, and I would love to see more organizations take that same approach. Don't wait for the EHR vendor and get ahead of their road map.

It means getting good at FHIR APIs, curating applications and solutions, and laying out a consistent innovation strategy aligned with your organization's goals. Government policy continues to move ahead on interoperability with standards, incentives, and requirements for EHR vendors. The stage is set for a wave of interconnected applications.

Jane Sarasohn-Kahn talks about the consumer's role in driving change in healthcare. There is a parallel with health IT leaders who are consumers of health technology. Health IT leaders can shape the health tech market for the upcoming ten to twenty years by exercising their power as health IT consumers. It is our nuclear power, the power of consumer choice. We can make our organizations and teams more innovative by purchasing cutting-edge and emerging solutions. We can change the way we work, and if our care model or reimbursement model changes, we can change our minds and go in a different direction.

Unvendoring is exercising our power as health IT purchasers and consumers. Let's harness this power and become innovative, dynamic, competitive, and futureproof. Start small, then go bigger.

Together, we'll unvendor healthcare.

Workbook

HEALTH IT LEADERS AS CAREGIVERS

Jane Sarasohn-Kahn sees IT leaders not just as health IT consumers, but also as health IT caregivers: "The health IT executive is a caregiver, for the patients in the institution, for the employees who are burned out because of the EHR, and they are also caregivers for our health system. Without those institutional caregivers there's no quintuple aim."[71] We need data and systems to help lower cost, to drive the experience, to drive the outcomes, to support clinician wellness and drive health equity.

Question: Exactly how do data and systems support each of the five quintuple aims? Think of one or two explicit examples for each of the goals. These can be current or future projects or applications in your organization.

---

71   Kedar Mate, "On the Quintuple Aim: Why Expand Beyond the Triple Aim?" Institute for Healthcare Improvement, February 4, 2022, https://www.ihi.org/insights/quintuple-aim-why-expand-beyond-triple-aim.

QUINTUPLE AIM	EXAMPLE OF DATA AND SYSTEMS IN SUPPORT OF THIS GOAL	EXAMPLE 2
Improve outcomes and population health		
Improve care experience		
Reduce cost		
Support clinician wellness		
Advance health equity		

Figure 16: How do your projects align with quintuple aim goals?

Circle the examples that require a more diverse IT stack. Are there specific unvendor scenarios that can help realize the quintuple aim objectives? Are you on a path to unvendor to achieve quintuple aim goals?

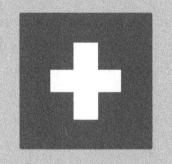

ACKNOWLEDGMENTS

I want to thank the many friends and colleagues who helped me talk through the ideas in this book: Subha Airan-Javia, Kyle Armstrong, Aneesh Chopra, Eve Cunningham, Michael Glickman, Luke Goetzke, Toyin Falola, Ken Kawamoto, Marty Lupinetti, Brett Marqard, David Muntz, Zeev Neuwirth, Nayan Patel, Jackson Rhoades, Evan Roberts, Jane Sarasohn-Kahn, Mark Scrimshire, Katherine Schneider, Larry Schunder, Rasu Shrestha, and Raj Toleti. Thank you for bringing your voices to the conversation.

Thanks to my colleagues at IT firms and health systems for helping me understand our industry and how technology supports care delivery: my friends at SMS, Siemens Health Services, Main Line Health, Thomas Jefferson University College of Population Health, Starbridge Advisors LLC, eClinicalWorks, HealthShare Exchange, Philips Wellcentive, AMIA, and HIMSS.

Thank you to the Forbes Books/Advantage team who helped me take this project from idea to print: Steve Johnson, Elizabeth Brueggemann, Elizabeth Kennedy, Heidi Scott, Alison Morse, Megan Elger, and Lauren McCarthy. Thank you, Karl Mooney, for the graphics.

Thank you to my running buddies, Jason Jackson, Andrew Gaess, John Dolan, Derek Dureka, and Dan Rosenak, for getting me unstuck.

Thank you to the Upper Dublin Public Library and its amazing staff for giving me a place to work.

And finally a bottom-of-my-heart thank-you to my family for supporting me throughout this project. Thank you, Titia, for your love, for your inspiration and insights, and for hiking the path of life with me. Thank you to our fun and exuberant kids and partners, Gerben and Ian, Mieke and Matt, Bart and Suzy. Quoting Ian's car license plate, URAWSME.

CONTACT ME

Tell me how your unvendor projects are going. I would love to highlight your projects, large and small, to the health IT community. Reach me on unvendor.us or at harm@scherpbier.health.

LIST OF ABBREVIATIONS

ACO Accountable Care Organization

AI Artificial Intelligence

API Application Program Interface

APM Alternative Payment Model

BI Business Intelligence

CBO Community-Based Organization

CCD Continuity of Care Document

CDS Clinical Decision Support

CGM Continuous Glucose Monitoring

CIE Community Information Exchange

CMS Centers for Medicare and Medicaid Services

CRM Customer Relationship Management

DS Decision Support

ED Emergency Department

EHR Electronic Health Record

ERX e-Prescribing

ETL Extract Transform Load

FHIR Fast Healthcare Interoperability Resources

HCAHPS	Hospital Consumer Assessment of Healthcare Providers and Systems
HIE	Health Information Exchange
HIM	Health Information Management
HIPAA	Health Insurance Portability and Accountability Act
HL7	Health Level 7
IT	Information Technology
ML	Machine Learning
MU	Meaningful Use
OAUTH	Open Authorization
ONC	Office of the National Coordinator for Health Information Technology
PCP	Primary Care Physician
PERS	Personal Emergency Response System
QHIN	Qualified Health Information Network
RCM	Revenue Cycle Management
ROI	Return on Investment
RPA	Robotic Process Automation
RPM	Remote Patient Monitoring
SDOH	Social Determinants of Health
TEFCA	Trusted Exchange Framework and Common Architecture
USCDI	United States Core Data for Interoperability
UI	User Interface
UX	User Experience
VBC	Value-Based Care
VOI	Value on Investment